LOTUS® 1-2-3®

— Release 5 for Windows™ —

SIMPLIFIED

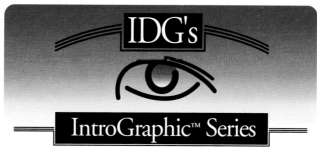

IDG's

IntroGraphic™ Series

by: maranGraphics' Development Group

IDG BOOKS

IDG Books Worldwide, Inc.
An International Data Group Company

San Mateo, California ✦ Indianapolis, Indiana ✦ Boston, Massachusetts

Lotus® 1-2-3® Release 5 for Windows™ Simplified

Published by
IDG Books Worldwide, Inc.
An International Data Group Company
155 Bovet Road, Suite 310
San Mateo, CA 94402
(415) 312-0650

Library of Congress Catalog Card No.: 94-079403
ISBN: 1-56884-670-3
Printed in the United States of America
10 9 8 7 6 5 4 3 2
Distributed in the United States by IDG Books Worldwide, Inc.

Distributed by Computer and Technical Books in Miami, Florida, for South America and the Caribbean; by Longman Singapore in Singapore, Malaysia, Thailand, and Korea; by Toppan Co. Ltd. in Japan; by Asia Computerworld in Hong Kong; by Woodslane Pty. Ltd. in Australia and New Zealand; and by Transworld Publishers Ltd. in the U.K. and Ireland.

For general information on IDG Books in the U.S., including information on discounts and premiums, contact IDG Books at 800-762-2974 or 317-895-5200.

For U.S. Corporate Sales and quantity discounts, contact maranGraphics at 800-469-6616, ext. 206.

For information on international sales of IDG Books, contact Christina Turner at 415-312-0633.

For information on translations, contact Marc Jeffrey Mikulich, Director of Foreign Subsidiary Rights, at IDG Books Worldwide. Fax Number 415-286-2747.

For sales inquiries and special prices for bulk quantities, write to the address above or call IDG Books Worldwide at 415-312-0650.

For information on using IDG Books in the classroom, or ordering examination copies, contact Jim Kelly at 800-434-2086.

Trademark Acknowledgments

©1994
maranGraphics, Inc.

The animated characters are the copyright of maranGraphics, Inc.

U.S. Corporate Sales	**U.S. Trade Sales**
Contact maranGraphics at (800) 469-6616, ext. 206 or Fax (905) 890-9434.	Contact IDG Books at (800) 434-3422 or (415) 312-0650.

About IDG Books Worldwide

Welcome to the world of IDG Books Worldwide.

IDG Books Worldwide, Inc., is a subsidiary of International Data Group, the world's largest publisher of business and computer-related information and the leading global provider of information services on information technology. IDG was founded more than 25 years ago and now employs more than 5,700 people worldwide. IDG publishes more than 200 computer publications in 63 countries (see listing below). Forty million people read one or more IDG publications each month.

Launched in 1990, IDG Books is today the fastest-growing publisher of computer and business books in the United States. We are proud to have received 3 awards from the Computer Press Association in recognition of editorial excellence, and our best-selling ...For Dummies series has more than 10 million copies in print with translations in more than 20 languages. IDG Books, through a recent joint venture with IDG's Hi-Tech Beijing, became the first U.S. publisher to publish a computer book in the People's Republic of China. In record time, IDG Books has become the first choice for millions of readers around the world who want to learn how to better manage their businesses.

Our mission is simple: Every IDG book is designed to bring extra value and skill-building instructions to the reader. Our books are written by experts who understand and care about our readers. The knowledge base of our editorial staff comes from years of experience in publishing, education, and journalism — experience which we use to produce books for the '90s. In short, we care about books, so we attract the best people. We devote special attention to details such as audience, interior design, use of icons, and illustrations. And because we use an efficient process of authoring, editing, and desktop publishing our books electronically, we can spend more time ensuring superior content and spend less time on the technicalities of making books.

You can count on our commitment to deliver high-quality books at competitive prices on topics customers want to read about. At IDG, we value quality, and we have been delivering quality for more than 25 years. You'll find no better book on a subject than an IDG book.

John Kilcullen
President and CEO
IDG Books Worldwide, Inc.

Credits

Author and Architect:
Ruth Maran

Copy Developer:
Kelleigh Wing

Technical Consultant:
Wendi Blouin Ewbank

Layout Artist:
Carol Walthers

Illustrator:
Dave Ross

Assistant Illustrator:
David de Haas

Screen Artist:
Christie Van Duin

Editors:
Colleen Cross
Judy Maran

Post Production:
Robert Maran

Acknowledgments

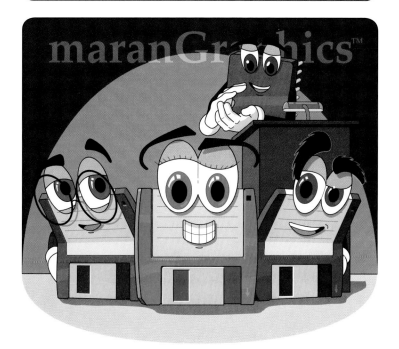

Many thanks to Marc LeBlanc of Lotus Development Corporation for his assistance and expert advice.

Special thanks to Wendi B. Ewbank for her insight and dedication in ensuring the technical accuracy of this book.

Thanks to Saverio C. Tropiano for his continuing support and consultation.

Thanks to the dedicated staff of maranGraphics, including Colleen Cross, David de Haas, Judy Maran, Maxine Maran, Robert Maran, Dave Ross, Christie Van Duin, Carol Walthers and Kelleigh Wing.

Finally, to Richard Maran who originated the easy-to-use graphic format of this guide. Thank you for your inspiration and guidance.

TABLE OF CONTENTS

INTRODUCTION TO LOTUS 1-2-3

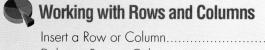

Working with Rows and Columns

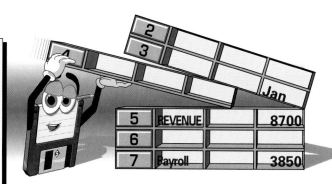

Format Your Worksheets

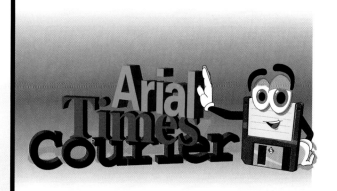

Print Your Worksheets

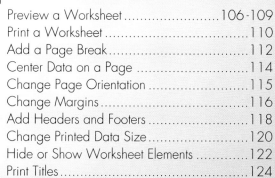

Change Your Screen Display

Using Multiple Worksheets

Using Multiple Files

Charting Data

Drawing Objects

Working With Databases

verview

GETTING STARTED

◆ In this chapter you will learn the basic skills needed to use Lotus 1-2-3.

Lotus® 1-2-3® for Windows™ is a spreadsheet program that will help you manage and analyze your data.

Getting Started	Save and Open Your Files	Edit Your Worksheets	Using Formulas and Functions	Working with Rows and Columns	Format Your Worksheets	Print Your Worksheets

- **Introduction**
- Using the Mouse
- Start 1-2-3
- Worksheet Basics
- Enter Data

- Enter Data Automatically
- Select Cells
- Select Commands
- Move Through a Worksheet
- Getting Help

HOW YOU CAN USE 1-2-3

PERSONAL FINANCES

1-2-3 helps you keep track of your mortgage, balance your checkbook, create a personal budget, compare investments and prepare your taxes.

FINANCIAL REPORTS

Businesses of all sizes use spreadsheets to analyze financial information. 1-2-3's formatting and charting features help you present your results in professional looking documents.

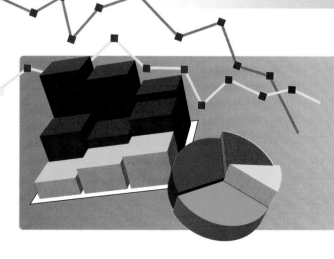

CHARTS

1-2-3 makes it easy to create charts from your spreadsheet data. Charts let you visually illustrate the relationship between different items.

3

The mouse is a hand-held device that lets you quickly select commands and perform tasks.

USING THE MOUSE

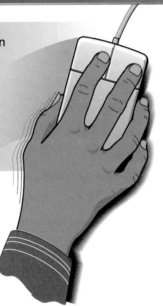

◆ Hold the mouse as shown in the diagram. Use your thumb and two rightmost fingers to guide the mouse while your two remaining fingers press the mouse buttons.

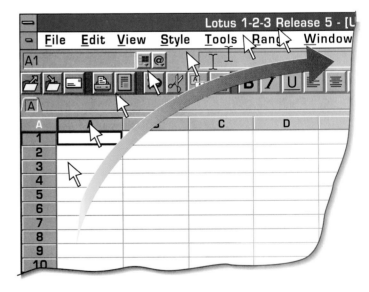

◆ When you move the mouse on your desk, the mouse pointer (▨ or I) on your screen moves in the same direction. The mouse pointer changes shape depending on its location on your screen and the action you are performing.

PARTS OF THE MOUSE

◆ The mouse has a left and right button. You can use these buttons to:

- open menus
- select commands
- choose options

Note: You will use the left button most of the time.

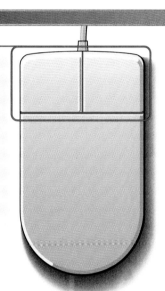

◆ Under the mouse is a ball that senses movement. To ensure smooth motion of the mouse, you should occasionally remove and clean this ball.

MOUSE TERMS

CLICK

Quickly press and release the left mouse button once.

DOUBLE-CLICK

Quickly press and release the left mouse button twice.

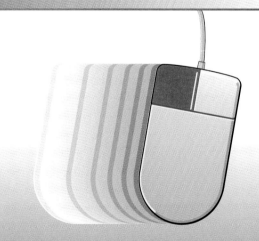

DRAG

When the mouse pointer (⬚ or I) is over an object on your screen, press and hold down the left mouse button and then move the mouse.

START 1-2-3

When you start 1-2-3, a blank worksheet appears. You can enter data into this worksheet.

START 1-2-3

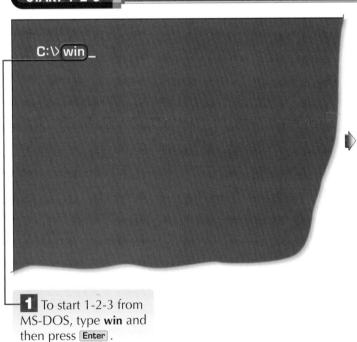

C:\> win _

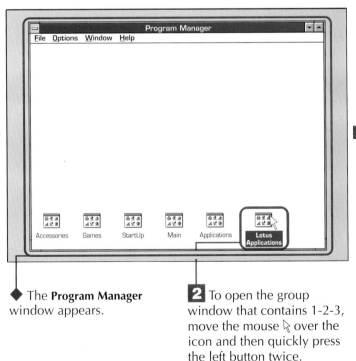

1 To start 1-2-3 from MS-DOS, type **win** and then press Enter.

◆ The **Program Manager** window appears.

2 To open the group window that contains 1-2-3, move the mouse ⌖ over the icon and then quickly press the left button twice.

Getting Started	Save and Open Your Files	Edit Your Worksheets	Using Formulas and Functions	Working with Rows and Columns	Format Your Worksheets	Print Your Worksheets

- Introduction
- Using the Mouse
- **Start 1-2-3**
- Worksheet Basics
- Enter Data

- Enter Data Automatically
- Select Cells
- Select Commands
- Move Through a Worksheet
- Getting Help

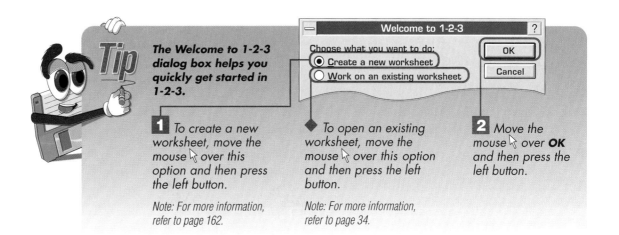

Tip

The Welcome to 1-2-3 dialog box helps you quickly get started in 1-2-3.

Welcome to 1-2-3

Choose what you want to do:
- ⦿ Create a new worksheet
- ○ Work on an existing worksheet

OK Cancel

1 To create a new worksheet, move the mouse ⫽ over this option and then press the left button.

Note: For more information, refer to page 162.

◆ To open an existing worksheet, move the mouse ⫽ over this option and then press the left button.

Note: For more information, refer to page 34.

2 Move the mouse ⫽ over **OK** and then press the left button.

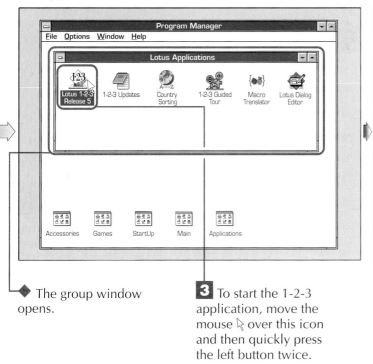

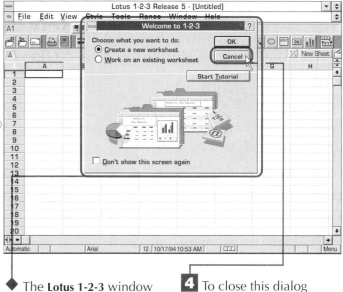

◆ The group window opens.

3 To start the 1-2-3 application, move the mouse ⫽ over this icon and then quickly press the left button twice.

◆ The **Lotus 1-2-3** window appears displaying a blank worksheet. The **Welcome to 1-2-3** dialog box also appears.

4 To close this dialog box, move the mouse ⫽ over **Cancel** and then press the left button.

WORKSHEET BASICS

A worksheet consists of columns, rows and cells.

COLUMNS, ROWS AND CELLS

Column

A column is a vertical line of boxes. 1-2-3 labels the columns in a worksheet (example: **F**).

Row

A row is a horizontal line of boxes. 1-2-3 numbers the rows in a worksheet (example: **8**).

Cell

A cell is the area where a column and row intersect (example: **F8**).

Getting Started	Save and Open Your Files	Edit Your Worksheets	Using Formulas and Functions	Working with Rows and Columns	Format Your Worksheets	Print Your Worksheets

- Introduction
- Using the Mouse
- Start 1-2-3
- **Worksheet Basics**
- Enter Data

- Enter Data Automatically
- Select Cells
- Select Commands
- Move Through a Worksheet
- Getting Help

> The current cell displays a thick border. You can only enter data into the current cell.

THE CURRENT CELL

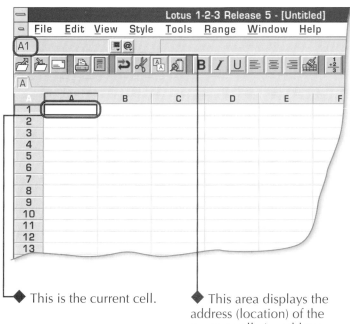

◆ This is the current cell.

◆ This area displays the address (location) of the current cell. An address consists of a column letter followed by a row number (example: **A1**).

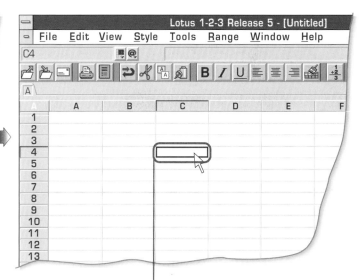

1 To make another cell on your screen the current cell, move the mouse ⟍ over the cell and then press the left button.

◆ The cell now displays a thick border.

ENTER DATA

You use your keyboard to enter data into the cells of your worksheet.

ENTER DATA

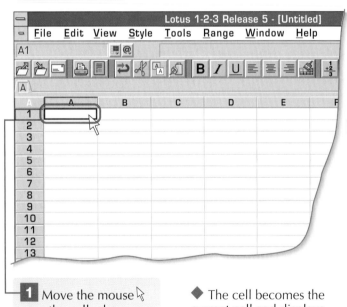

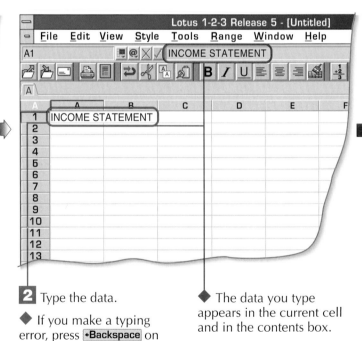

1 Move the mouse ⍨ over the cell where you want to enter data (example: **A1**) and then press the left button.

◆ The cell becomes the current cell and displays a thick border.

2 Type the data.

◆ If you make a typing error, press **◆Backspace** on your keyboard to remove the incorrect data and then retype.

◆ The data you type appears in the current cell and in the contents box.

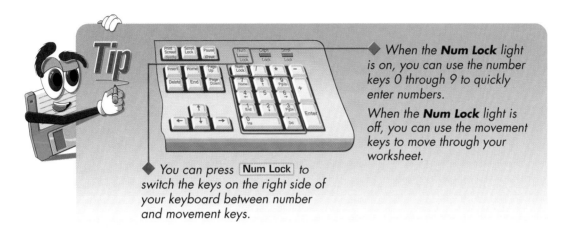

Tip

When the **Num Lock** light is on, you can use the number keys 0 through 9 to quickly enter numbers.

When the **Num Lock** light is off, you can use the movement keys to move through your worksheet.

◆ You can press `Num Lock` to switch the keys on the right side of your keyboard between number and movement keys.

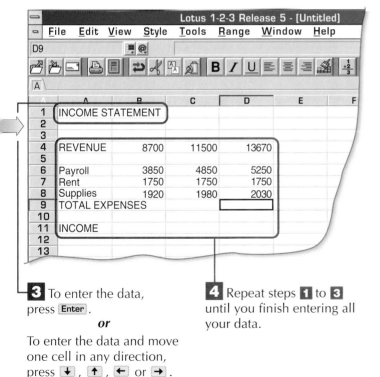

3 To enter the data, press `Enter`.

or

To enter the data and move one cell in any direction, press ⬇ , ⬆ , ⬅ or ➡ .

4 Repeat steps **1** to **3** until you finish entering all your data.

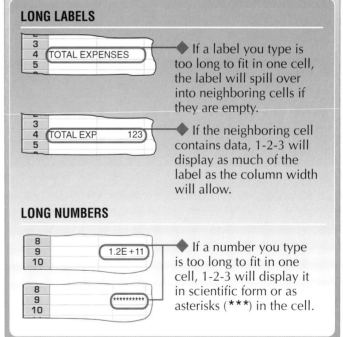

LONG LABELS

◆ If a label you type is too long to fit in one cell, the label will spill over into neighboring cells if they are empty.

◆ If the neighboring cell contains data, 1-2-3 will display as much of the label as the column width will allow.

LONG NUMBERS

◆ If a number you type is too long to fit in one cell, 1-2-3 will display it in scientific form or as asterisks (*******) in the cell.

Note: To display an entire label or number, you must increase the column width. For more information, refer to page 76.

11

ENTER DATA AUTOMATICALLY

1-2-3 can save you time by completing a series of labels or numbers in your worksheet.

ENTER DATA AUTOMATICALLY

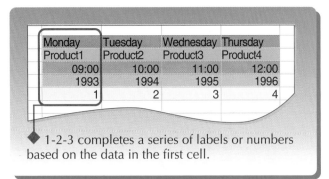

Monday	Tuesday	Wednesday	Thursday
Product1	Product2	Product3	Product4
09:00	10:00	11:00	12:00
1993	1994	1995	1996
1	2	3	4

◆ 1-2-3 completes a series of labels or numbers based on the data in the first cell.

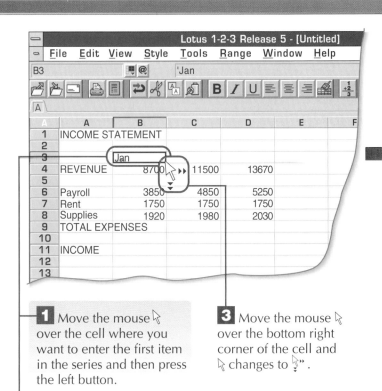

1 Move the mouse over the cell where you want to enter the first item in the series and then press the left button.

2 Type the first item in the series (example: **Jan**) and then press Enter.

3 Move the mouse over the bottom right corner of the cell and changes to .

12

| Getting Started | Save and Open Your Files | Edit Your Worksheets | Using Formulas and Functions | Working with Rows and Columns | Format Your Worksheets | Print Your Worksheets |

- Introduction
- Using the Mouse
- Start 1-2-3
- Worksheet Basics
- Enter Data

- **Enter Data Automatically**
- Select Cells
- Select Commands
- Move Through a Worksheet
- Getting Help

Tip

You can create a series that increases by more than one unit.

January	April	July	October
Monday	Wednesday	Friday	Sunday
5	10	15	20
1990	1992	1994	1996

1 Type and enter the first two labels or numbers in the series.

2 Select the cells containing the first two labels or numbers.

Note: To select cells, refer to page 14.

3 Perform steps **3** to **5** below.

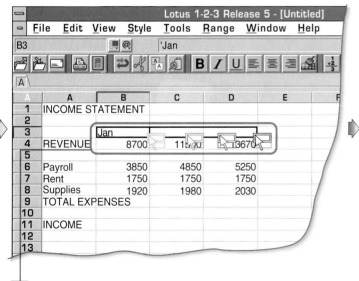

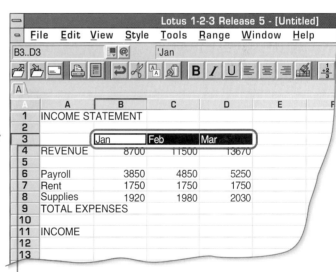

4 Press and hold down the left button as you drag the mouse over the cells you want to include in the series.

5 Release the button and the cells display the series.

Note: You can also enter data automatically in columns.

13

SELECT CELLS

Before you can use many 1-2-3 features, you must first select the cells you want to work with. Selected cells are called a range and appear highlighted on your screen.

SELECT A ROW

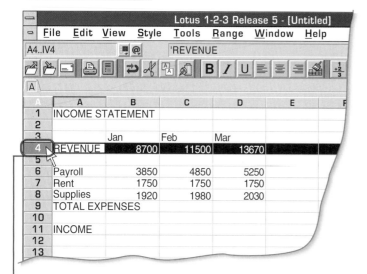

1 Move the mouse ⇦ over the row number you want to select (example: **4**) and then press the left button.

◆ Make sure the mouse looks like ⇦ (not ✛) before pressing the button.

TO CANCEL A SELECTION

Move the mouse ⇦ over any cell in your worksheet and then press the left button.

SELECT A COLUMN

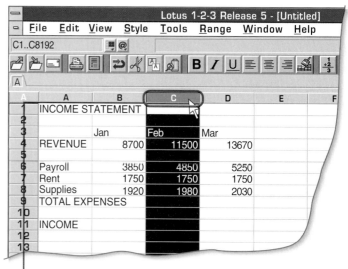

1 Move the mouse ⇦ over the column letter you want to select (example: **C**) and then press the left button.

◆ Make sure the mouse looks like ⇦ (not ✛) before pressing the button.

INTRODUCTION TO LOTUS 1-2-3

| Getting Started | Save and Open Your Files | Edit Your Worksheets | Using Formulas and Functions | Working with Rows and Columns | Format Your Worksheets | Print Your Worksheets |

- Introduction
- Using the Mouse
- Start 1-2-3
- Worksheet Basics
- Enter Data

- Enter Data Automatically
- **Select Cells**
- Select Commands
- Move Through a Worksheet
- Getting Help

SELECT THE ENTIRE WORKSHEET

1 Move the mouse over the area where the row and column headings intersect and then press the left button.

SELECT A GROUP OF CELLS

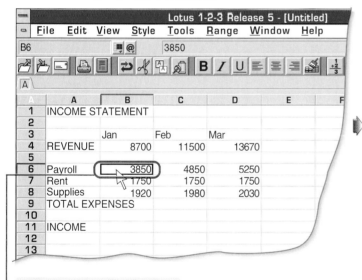

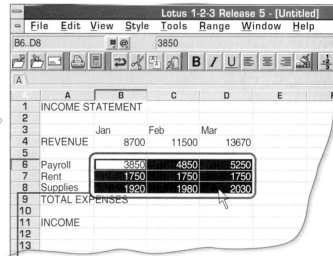

1 Move the mouse over the first cell you want to select (example: **B6**) and then press and hold down the left button.

2 Still holding down the button, drag the mouse until you highlight all the cells you want to select.

3 Release the button.

SELECT TWO GROUPS OF CELLS

To select another group of cells, press and hold down Ctrl while repeating steps **1** to **3**.

SELECT COMMANDS

You can open a menu to display a list of related commands. You can then select the command you want to use.

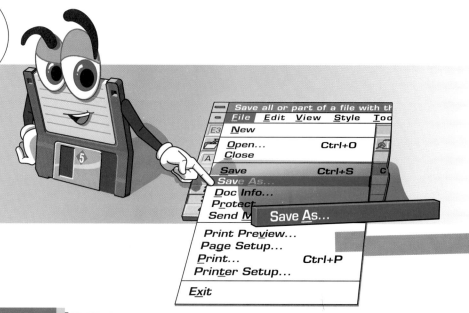

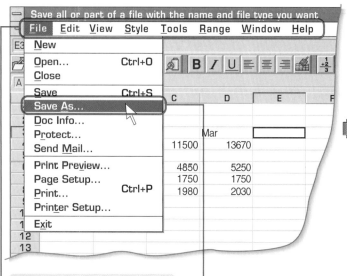

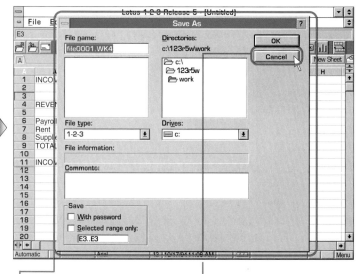

1 To open a menu, move the mouse ⌖ over the menu name (example: **File**) and then press the left button.

Note: To close a menu, move the mouse ⌖ over your worksheet and then press the left button.

2 To select a command, move the mouse ⌖ over the command name (example: **Save As**) and then press the left button.

◆ A dialog box appears if 1-2-3 requires more information to carry out the command.

3 To close a dialog box, move the mouse ⌖ over **Cancel** and then press the left button.

16

INTRODUCTION TO LOTUS 1-2-3

Getting Started	Save and Open Your Files	Edit Your Worksheets	Using Formulas and Functions	Working with Rows and Columns	Format Your Worksheets	Print Your Worksheets

- Introduction
- Using the Mouse
- Start 1-2-3
- Worksheet Basics
- Enter Data

- Enter Data Automatically
- Select Cells
- **Select Commands**
- Move Through a Worksheet
- Getting Help

Tips

```
File
New
Open...        Ctrl+O
Close
Save           Ctrl+S
Save As...
Doc Info...
Protect...
```

◆ Some commands display a keyboard shortcut. For example, press Ctrl + S to select the **Save** command.

>Click<   >Click<

◆ If key names are separated by a plus sign (+), press and hold down the first key before pressing the second key (example: Ctrl + S).

USING THE MENUS WITH THE KEYBOARD

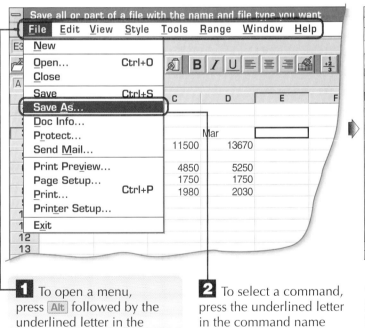

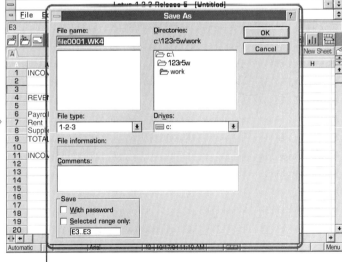

1 To open a menu, press Alt followed by the underlined letter in the menu name (example: F for **File**).

Note: To close a menu, press Alt .

2 To select a command, press the underlined letter in the command name (example: A for **Save As**).

◆ A dialog box appears if 1-2-3 requires more information to carry out the command.

3 To close a dialog box, press Esc .

SELECT COMMANDS

You can use the SmartIcons to quickly select the most commonly used commands.

USING THE SMARTICONS

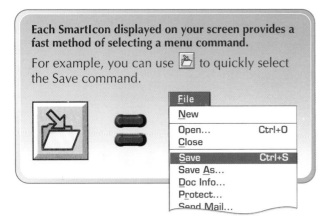

Each SmartIcon displayed on your screen provides a fast method of selecting a menu command.

For example, you can use 📂 to quickly select the Save command.

File	
New	
Open...	Ctrl+O
Close	
Save	Ctrl+S
Save As...	
Doc Info...	
Protect...	
Send Mail...	

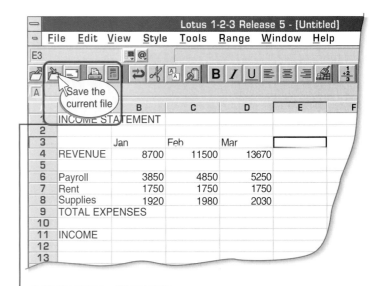

1 Move the mouse ⟍ over a SmartIcon of interest (example: 📂).

◆ A description of the SmartIcon appears.

2 To select the SmartIcon, press the left button.

Getting Started	Save and Open Your Files	Edit Your Worksheets	Using Formulas and Functions	Working with Rows and Columns	Format Your Worksheets	Print Your Worksheets

- Introduction
- Using the Mouse
- Start 1-2-3
- Worksheet Basics
- Enter Data

- Enter Data Automatically
- Select Cells
- **Select Commands**
- Move Through a Worksheet
- Getting Help

> A quick menu displays a list of commonly used commands for an area you select.

USING THE QUICK MENUS

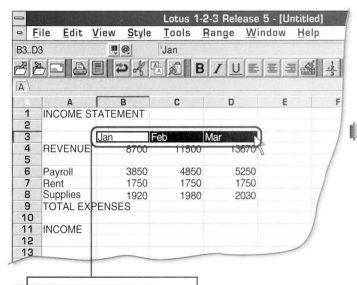

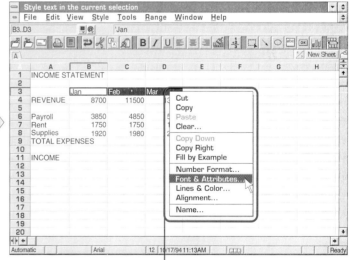

1 Select the cells containing the data you want to work with.

Note: To select cells, refer to page 14.

2 Move the mouse ⬚ anywhere over the cells you selected and then press the **right** button.

◆ A quick menu appears.

3 Move the mouse ⬚ over the command you want to use and then press the left button.

Note: To close a quick menu, move the mouse ⬚ outside the menu and then press the left button.

MOVE THROUGH A WORKSHEET

If your worksheet contains a lot of data, your computer screen cannot display all of the data at the same time. You must scroll through the worksheet to view other areas.

MOVE ONE CELL IN ANY DIRECTION

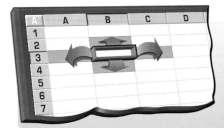

→ Press this key to move **right** one cell.

← Press this key to move **left** one cell.

↓ Press this key to move **down** one cell.

↑ Press this key to move **up** one cell.

MOVE TO CELL A1

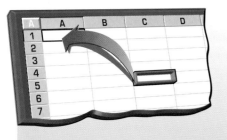

◆ Press `Home` to move to cell **A1** from any cell in your worksheet.

MOVE ONE SCREEN UP OR DOWN

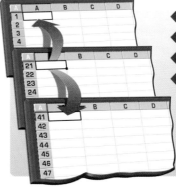

◆ Press `PageDown` to move **down** one screen.

◆ Press `PageUp` to move **up** one screen.

◆ Press `Ctrl` + → to move **right** one screen.

◆ Press `Ctrl` + ← to move **left** one screen.

| Getting Started | Save and Open Your Files | Edit Your Worksheets | Using Formulas and Functions | Working with Rows and Columns | Format Your Worksheets | Print Your Worksheets |

- Introduction
- Using the Mouse
- Start 1-2-3
- Worksheet Basics
- Enter Data

- Enter Data Automatically
- Select Cells
- Select Commands
- **Move Through a Worksheet**
- Getting Help

SCROLL UP OR DOWN

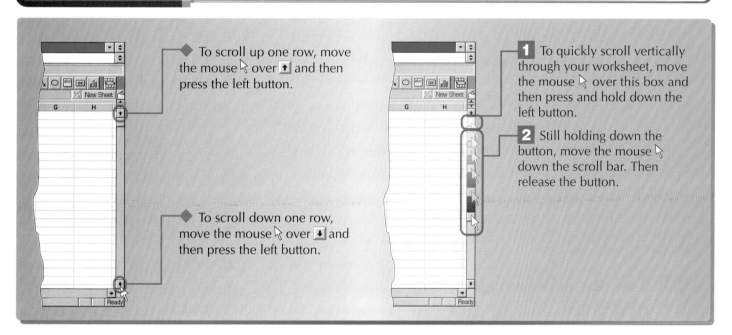

◆ To scroll up one row, move the mouse ⌖ over ⬆ and then press the left button.

◆ To scroll down one row, move the mouse ⌖ over ⬇ and then press the left button.

1 To quickly scroll vertically through your worksheet, move the mouse ⌖ over this box and then press and hold down the left button.

2 Still holding down the button, move the mouse ⌖ down the scroll bar. Then release the button.

SCROLL LEFT OR RIGHT

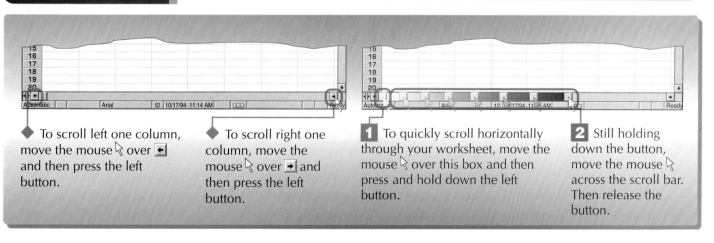

◆ To scroll left one column, move the mouse ⌖ over ◀ and then press the left button.

◆ To scroll right one column, move the mouse ⌖ over ▶ and then press the left button.

1 To quickly scroll horizontally through your worksheet, move the mouse ⌖ over this box and then press and hold down the left button.

2 Still holding down the button, move the mouse ⌖ across the scroll bar. Then release the button.

GETTING HELP

If you forget how to perform a task, you can use the Help feature to obtain information. This can save you time by eliminating the need to refer to other sources.

GETTING HELP

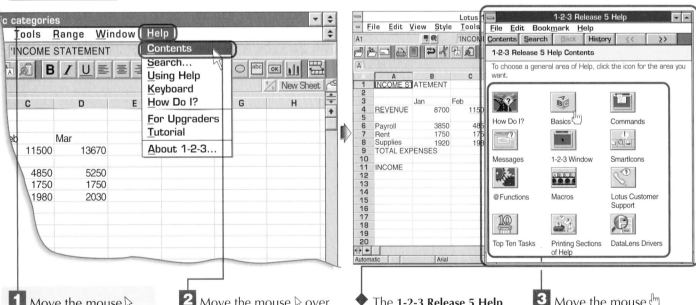

1 Move the mouse over **Help** and then press the left button.

2 Move the mouse over **Contents** and then press the left button.

◆ The **1-2-3 Release 5 Help** window appears.

3 Move the mouse over a category of interest (example: **Basics**) and then press the left button.

Getting Started	Save and Open Your Files	Edit Your Worksheets	Using Formulas and Functions	Working with Rows and Columns	Format Your Worksheets	Print Your Worksheets

- Introduction
- Using the Mouse
- Start 1-2-3
- Worksheet Basics
- Enter Data

- Enter Data Automatically
- Select Cells
- Select Commands
- Move Through a Worksheet
- **Getting Help**

Tip

In the Help window, you can display information about text that appears in green type.

Entering Data

◆ If text appears with a solid underline, you can display related information about the term.

mouse pointer

◆ If text appears with a dotted underline, you can display a definition of the term.

Note: To display the information, move the mouse over the text and then press the left button.

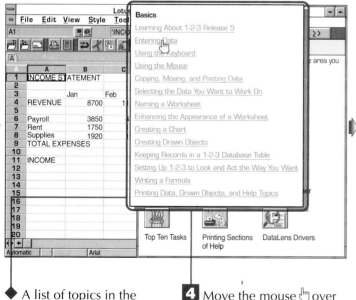

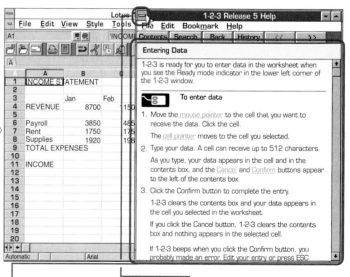

◆ A list of topics in the category you selected appears.

4 Move the mouse over a topic of interest (example: **Entering Data**) and then press the left button.

◆ A detailed explanation of the topic you selected appears.

5 To close the **Help** window, move the mouse over ⊟ and then quickly press the left button twice.

verview

SAVE AND OPEN YOUR FILES

Introduction

Save a File

Save a File to a Diskette

Exit 1-2-3

Open a File

Password Protect a File

◆ In this chapter you will learn how to save your work and exit 1-2-3. You will also learn how to open and password protect your files.

INTRODUCTION

Hard Drive (C:)

The hard drive stores your programs and data. It contains many directories to organize your information.

Files

1-2-3 stores your worksheets as files.

Your computer stores programs and data in devices called drives. A drive contains directories to organize your information. Think of a drive as a filing cabinet and directories as drawers and folders.

Directories

A directory usually contains related information. For example, the **123r5w** directory contains the Lotus 1-2-3 files.

Getting Started	Save and Open Your Files	Edit Your Worksheets	Using Formulas and Functions	Working with Rows and Columns	Format Your Worksheets	Print Your Worksheets

- **Introduction**
- Save a File
- Save a File to a Diskette
- Exit 1-2-3
- Open a File
- Password Protect a File

Most computers have one hard drive and one or two floppy drives to store information.

Hard drive (C:)

◆ The hard drive magnetically stores information inside your computer. It is called drive **C**.

*Note: Your computer may be set up to have additional hard drives (example: drive **D**).*

Floppy drives (A: and B:)

◆ A floppy drive stores information on removable diskettes (or floppy disks). A diskette operates slower and stores less data than a hard drive.

◆ **Diskettes are used to:**

- Load new programs.
- Store backup copies of data.
- Transfer data to other computers.

If your computer has only one floppy drive, it is called drive **A**.

If your computer has two floppy drives, the second drive is called drive **B**.

27

SAVE A FILE

You should save your file to store it for future use. This lets you later retrieve the file for reviewing or editing purposes.

SAVE A FILE

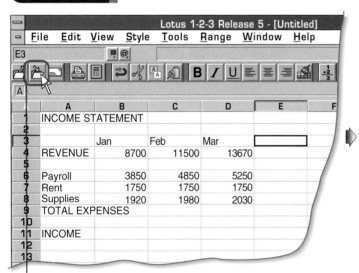

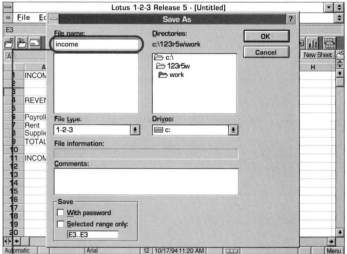

1 Move the mouse ⌖ over 🖫 and then press the left button.

◆ The **Save As** dialog box appears.

*Note: If you previously saved your file, the **Save As** dialog box will **not** appear since you have already named the file.*

2 Type a name for your file (example: **income**).

*Note: To make it easier to find your file later on, do not type an extension. 1-2-3 will automatically add the **wk4** extension to the file name.*

Rules for Naming a File

A file name *can* contain the following characters:

◆ The letters A to Z, upper or lower case

◆ The numbers 0 to 9

◆ The symbols
_ ^ # ~ ! # % & { } @ ( )

A file name *cannot* contain the following characters:

◆ A period (.)

◆ A comma (,)

◆ A blank space

◆ The symbols
+ = \ / ? < > *

Each file in a directory must have a unique name.

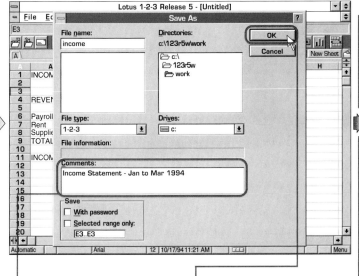

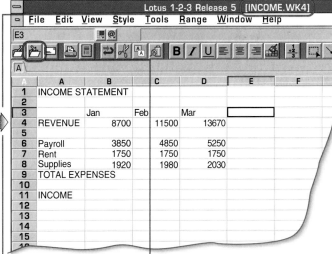

3 To enter information about the file, move the mouse I over this area and then press the left button. Then type the text.

Note: The information you enter will help you identify the file later on.

4 Move the mouse ⌖ over **OK** and then press the left button.

◆ 1-2-3 saves your file and displays the name at the top of your screen.

◆ You should save your file every 5 to 10 minutes to store any changes made since the last time you saved the file. To save changes, move the mouse ⌖ over 🖫 and then press the left button.

SAVE A FILE TO A DISKETTE

If you want to give your colleagues a copy of a file, you can save the file to a diskette. They can then review the file on their own computers.

SAVE A FILE TO A DISKETTE

1 Insert a diskette into a floppy drive (example: **drive a**).

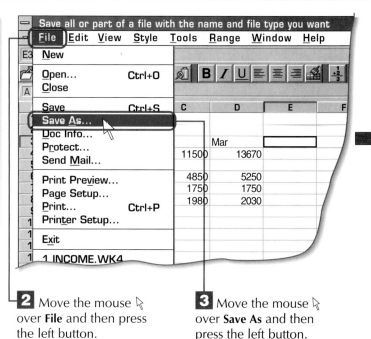

2 Move the mouse ℝ over **File** and then press the left button.

3 Move the mouse ℝ over **Save As** and then press the left button.

Getting Started	Save and Open Your Files	Edit Your Worksheets	Using Formulas and Functions	Working with Rows and Columns	Format Your Worksheets	Print Your Worksheets

- Introduction
- Save a File
- **Save a File to a Diskette**
- Exit 1-2-3
- Open a File
- Password Protect a File

SAVE A FILE WITH A NEW NAME

After you save your file, you may want to make additional changes. In case you regret any of these changes, you can keep a copy of the old version by saving the file with a new name.

1 Perform steps **2** to **4** below.

2 Move the mouse ↳ over **OK** and then press the left button.

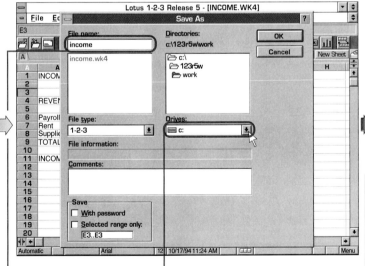

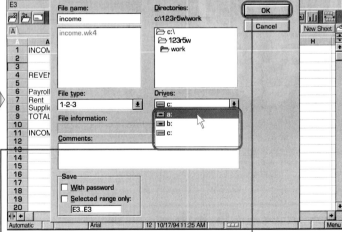

◆ The **Save As** dialog box appears.

4 The **File name:** box displays the current file name. To save your file with a different name, type a new name.

◆ The **Drives:** box displays the current drive (example: **c:**).

5 To save the file to a different drive, move the mouse ↳ over ▼ in the **Drives:** box and then press the left button.

◆ A list of the available drives for your computer appears.

6 Move the mouse ↳ over the drive you want to use (example: **a:**) and then press the left button.

7 To save your file, move the mouse ↳ over **OK** and then press the left button.

EXIT 1-2-3

When you finish using 1-2-3, you can exit the program to return to the Windows Program Manager.

EXIT 1-2-3

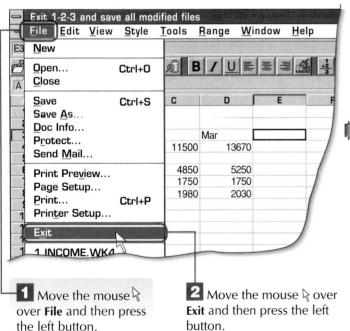

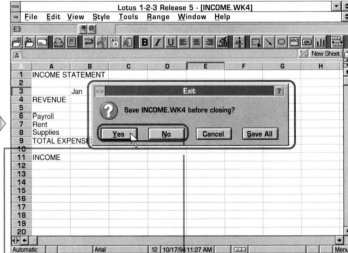

1 Move the mouse ⌖ over **File** and then press the left button.

2 Move the mouse ⌖ over **Exit** and then press the left button.

◆ This dialog box appears if you have not saved changes made to your file.

3 To save your file before exiting, move the mouse ⌖ over **Yes** and then press the left button.

◆ To exit without saving your file, move the mouse ⌖ over **No** and then press the left button.

Getting Started	Save and Open Your Files	Edit Your Worksheets	Using Formulas and Functions	Working with Rows and Columns	Format Your Worksheets	Print Your Worksheets

- Introduction
- Save a File
- Save a File to a Diskette
- **Exit 1-2-3**
- Open a File
- Password Protect a File

IMPORTANT!

You must always exit 1-2-3 and Windows before turning off your computer. Failure to do so may result in damage or loss of valuable information.

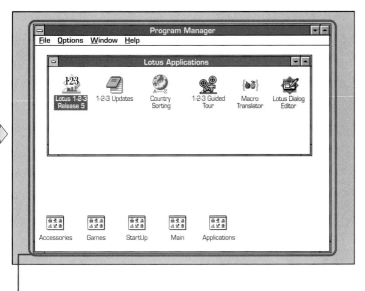

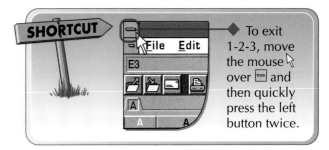

SHORTCUT

◆ To exit 1-2-3, move the mouse over ⊟ and then quickly press the left button twice.

◆ The **Program Manager** window appears.

Note: To restart 1-2-3, refer to page 6.

OPEN A FILE

You can open a saved file and display it on your screen. This lets you review and edit your work.

OPEN A FILE

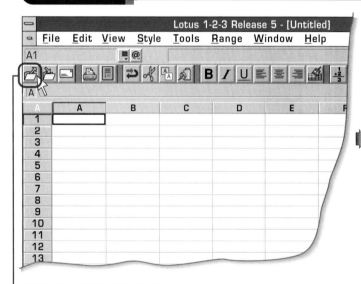

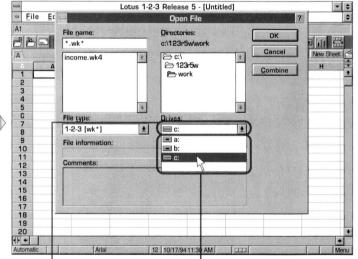

1 Move the mouse ▷ over 📁 and then press the left button.

◆ The **Open File** dialog box appears.

◆ The **Drives:** box displays the current drive (example: **c:**).

2 To open a file on a different drive, move the mouse ▷ over ⬇ in the **Drives:** box and then press the left button.

◆ A list of the available drives for your computer appears.

3 Move the mouse ▷ over the drive containing the file you want to open and then press the left button.

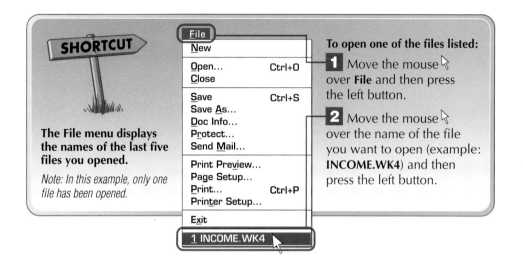

SHORTCUT

The File menu displays the names of the last five files you opened.

Note: In this example, only one file has been opened.

File menu items:
New
Open... Ctrl+O
Close
Save Ctrl+S
Save As...
Doc Info...
Protect...
Send Mail...
Print Preview...
Page Setup...
Print... Ctrl+P
Printer Setup...
Exit
1 INCOME.WK4

To open one of the files listed:

1 Move the mouse over **File** and then press the left button.

2 Move the mouse over the name of the file you want to open (example: **INCOME.WK4**) and then press the left button.

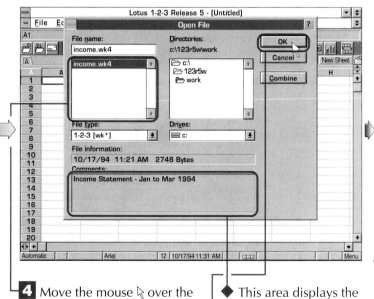

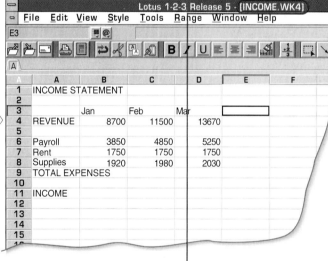

4 Move the mouse over the name of the file you want to open (example: **income.wk4**) and then press the left button.

◆ This area displays the text you entered when you saved the file.

5 Move the mouse over **OK** and then press the left button.

◆ 1-2-3 opens the file and displays it on your screen. You can now make changes to the file.

◆ The name of the file appears at the top of your screen.

35

PASSWORD PROTECT A FILE

You can stop other people from opening your file by protecting it with a password.

PASSWORD PROTECT A FILE

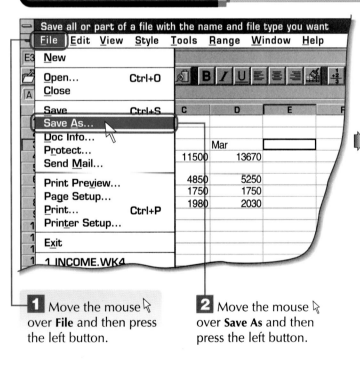

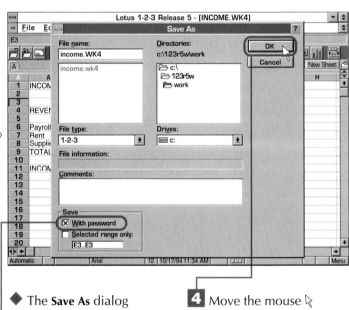

1 Move the mouse over **File** and then press the left button.

2 Move the mouse over **Save As** and then press the left button.

◆ The **Save As** dialog box appears.

3 Move the mouse over **With password** and then press the left button (□ changes to ⊠).

4 Move the mouse over **OK** and then press the left button.

Getting Started	Save and Open Your Files	Edit Your Worksheets	Using Formulas and Functions	Working with Rows and Columns	Format Your Worksheets	Print Your Worksheets

- Introduction
- Save a File
- Save a File to a Diskette
- Exit 1-2-3
- Open a File
- **Password Protect a File**

Tip

When you try to open a password protected file, this dialog box appears.

To open the file, type the password and then press `Enter` on your keyboard.

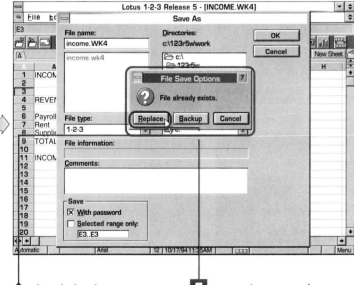

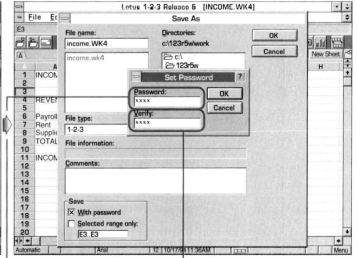

◆ This dialog box appears if you previously saved your file.

5 Move the mouse ⌖ over **Replace** and then press the left button.

6 Type the password you want to use. 1-2-3 displays a symbol (**x**) for each character you type.

*Note: Passwords are case sensitive. For example, if your password is **Car** you cannot type **car** or **CAR** to open the file.*

7 To confirm the password, press `Tab` to move to the **Verify:** box.

8 Type the password again and then press `Enter`.

*Note: To remove the password, perform steps **1** to **5**.*

37

verview

EDIT YOUR WORKSHEETS

Edit Data

Delete Data

Undo Last Change

Move Data

Copy Data

Check Spelling

◆ In this chapter you will learn how to make changes to data in your worksheet.

EDIT DATA

After you enter data into your worksheet, you can correct a typing error or revise the data.

EDIT DATA IN A CELL

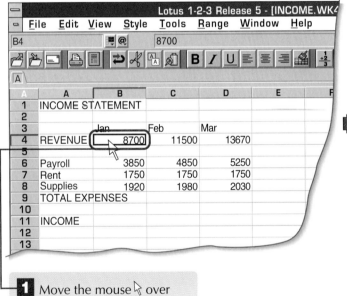

1 Move the mouse ⌖ over the cell containing the data you want to change (example: **B4**) and then quickly press the left button twice.

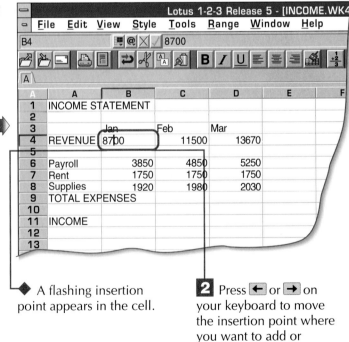

◆ A flashing insertion point appears in the cell.

2 Press ← or → on your keyboard to move the insertion point where you want to add or delete characters.

40

INTRODUCTION TO LOTUS 1-2-3

| Getting Started | Save and Open Your Files | Edit Your Worksheets | Using Formulas and Functions | Working with Rows and Columns | Format Your Worksheets | Print Your Worksheets |

- **Edit Data**
- Delete Data
- Undo Last Change
- Move Data
- Copy Data
- Check Spelling

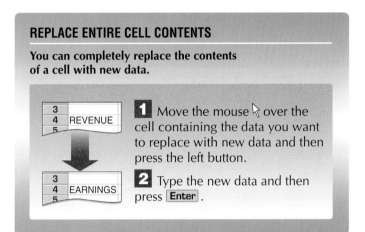

REPLACE ENTIRE CELL CONTENTS

You can completely replace the contents of a cell with new data.

1 Move the mouse ⬚ over the cell containing the data you want to replace with new data and then press the left button.

2 Type the new data and then press **Enter** .

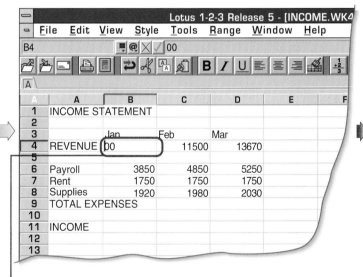

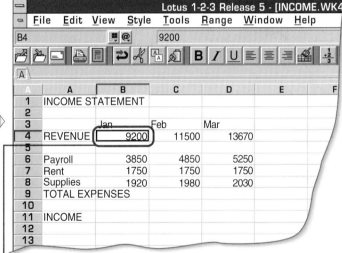

3 To remove the character to the left of the insertion point, press **←Backspace** .

◆ To remove the character to the right of the insertion point, press **Delete** .

4 To insert data where the insertion point flashes on your screen, type the data.

5 When you finish making the changes, press **Enter** .

DELETE UNDO
DATA LAST CHANGE

You can completely erase the contents of cells in your worksheet.

DELETE DATA

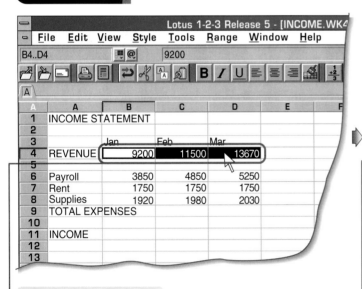

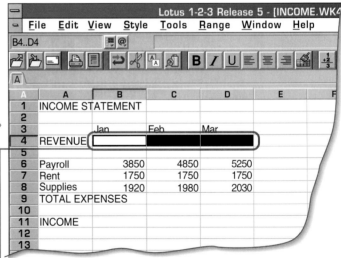

1 Select the cells containing the data you want to remove.

Note: To select cells, refer to page 14.

2 Press **Delete** and the data in the cells you selected disappears.

42

Getting
Started

Save and
Open Your
Files

**Edit Your
Worksheets**

Using
Formulas
and Functions

Working with
Rows and
Columns

Format Your
Worksheets

Print Your
Worksheets

• Edit Data
• **Delete Data**
• **Undo Last Change**
• Move Data
• Copy Data
• Check Spelling

> 1-2-3 remembers
> the last change you
> made to your worksheet.
> If you regret this change,
> you can cancel it by
> immediately using the
> Undo feature.

UNDO YOUR LAST CHANGE

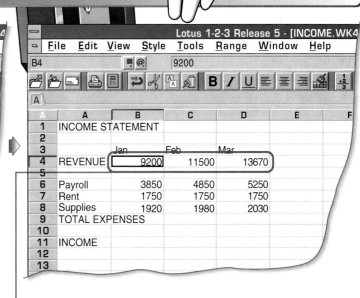

1 To cancel the last change made to your worksheet, move the mouse ⌖ over ⮌ and then press the left button.

◆ 1-2-3 cancels your last change.

Note: In this example, 1-2-3 restores the data you deleted.

43

MOVE DATA

You can move data from one location in your worksheet to another. 1-2-3 cuts the data and pastes it in a new location. The original data disappears.

MOVE DATA

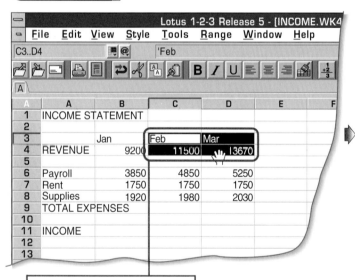

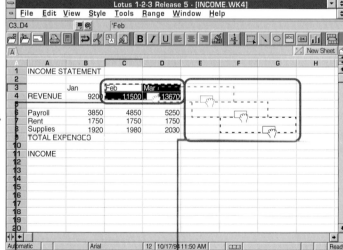

1 Select the cells containing the data you want to move to a new location.

Note: To select cells, refer to page 14.

2 Move the mouse ⇧ over a border of the selected cells (⇧ changes to ✋).

3 Press and hold down the left button (✋ changes to ☞).

4 Still holding down the left button, drag the mouse ☞ where you want to place the data.

◆ A dotted rectangular box indicates where the data will appear.

Getting Started	Save and Open Your Files	Edit Your Worksheets	Using Formulas and Functions	Working with Rows and Columns	Format Your Worksheets	Print Your Worksheets

Edit Your Worksheets

- Edit Data
- Delete Data
- Undo Last Change
- **Move Data**
- Copy Data
- Check Spelling

You can also move data to another worksheet.

Note: For more information, refer to page 144.

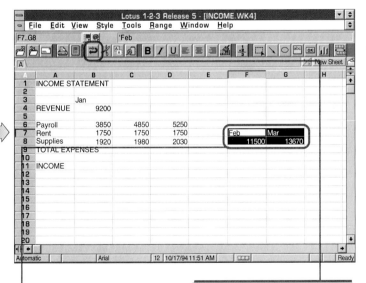

5 Release the left button and the data moves to the new location.

CANCEL THE MOVE

◆ To immediately cancel the move, position the mouse ⬚ over ⬚ and then press the left button.

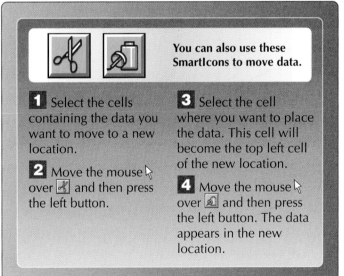

You can also use these SmartIcons to move data.

1 Select the cells containing the data you want to move to a new location.

2 Move the mouse over ✄ and then press the left button.

3 Select the cell where you want to place the data. This cell will become the top left cell of the new location.

4 Move the mouse over ⬚ and then press the left button. The data appears in the new location.

COPY DATA

You can copy data from one location in your worksheet to another. 1-2-3 copies the data and pastes it in a new location. The original data remains in its place.

COPY DATA

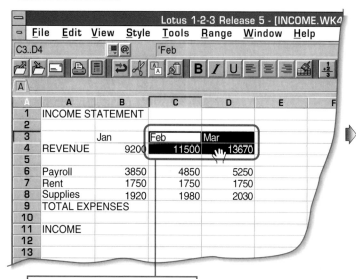

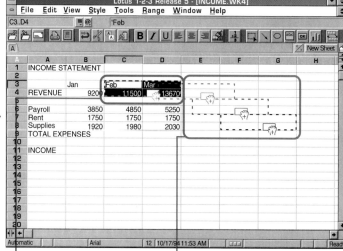

1 Select the cells containing the data you want to copy to a new location.

Note: To select cells, refer to page 14.

2 Move the mouse ⬐ over a border of the selected cells (⬐ changes to ✋).

3 Press and hold down `Ctrl` and the left button (✋ changes to 🖐).

4 Still holding down `Ctrl` and the left button, drag the mouse 🖐 where you want to place the copy.

◆ A dotted rectangular box indicates where the data will appear.

Getting Started	Save and Open Your Files	**Edit Your Worksheets**	Using Formulas and Functions	Working with Rows and Columns	Format Your Worksheets	Print Your Worksheets

- Edit Data
- Delete Data
- Undo Last Change
- Move Data
- **Copy Data**
- Check Spelling

You can also copy data to another worksheet.

Note: For more information, refer to page 144.

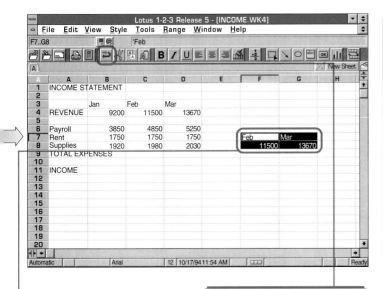

5 Release the left button and then release **Ctrl**.

◆ A copy of the data appears in the new location.

CANCEL THE COPY

◆ To immediately cancel the copy, move the mouse ⌖ over and then press the left button.

You can also use these SmartIcons to copy data.

1 Select the cells containing the data you want to copy to a new location.

2 Move the mouse ⌖ over ▣ and then press the left button.

3 Select the cell where you want to place the data. This cell will become the top left cell of the new location.

4 Move the mouse ⌖ over ▣ and then press the left button. A copy of the data appears in the new location.

*Note: You can repeat steps **3** and **4** to place the data in multiple locations in your worksheet.*

47

CHECK SPELLING

You can use the Spelling feature to find and correct spelling errors in your worksheet.

1-2-3 compares every word in your worksheet to words in its own dictionary. If a word does not exist in the dictionary, 1-2-3 considers it misspelled.

SUPLIES

SUPPLIES

Lotus Dictionary
Expanded 5.0 Version

CHECK SPELLING

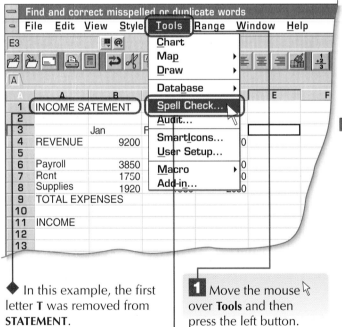

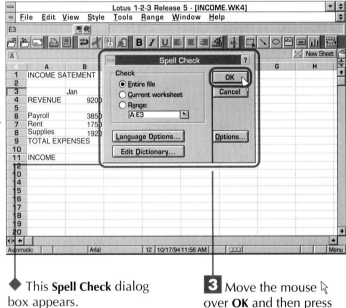

◆ In this example, the first letter **T** was removed from **STATEMENT**.

Note: To spell check a section of your worksheet, select the cells before performing step **1**. *To select cells, refer to page 14.*

1 Move the mouse over **Tools** and then press the left button.

2 Move the mouse over **Spell Check** and then press the left button.

◆ This **Spell Check** dialog box appears.

3 Move the mouse over **OK** and then press the left button.

Getting
Started

Save and
Open Your
Files

**Edit Your
Worksheets**

Using
Formulas
and Functions

Working with
Rows and
Columns

Format Your
Worksheets

Print Your
Worksheets

- Edit Data
- Delete Data
- Undo Last Change
- Move Data
- Copy Data
- **Check Spelling**

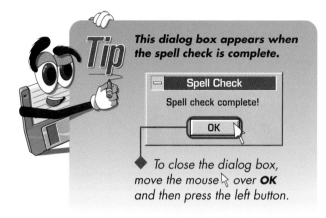

**This dialog box appears when
the spell check is complete.**

Spell Check

Spell check complete!

OK

◆ To close the dialog box,
move the mouse ₖ over **OK**
and then press the left button.

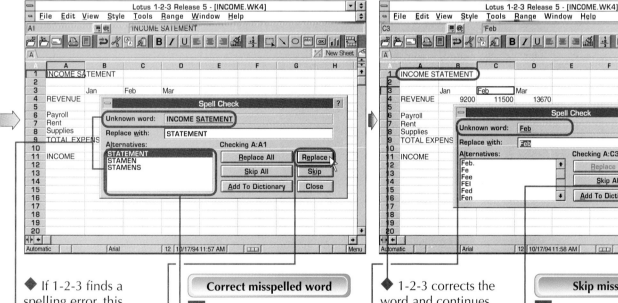

◆ If 1-2-3 finds a
spelling error, this
Spell Check dialog
box appears.

◆ 1-2-3 displays
the word it does
not recognize and
suggestions to correct
the error.

Correct misspelled word

4 To correct the spelling,
move the mouse ₖ over the
word you want to use and
then press the left button.

5 Move the mouse ₖ over
Replace and then press the
left button.

◆ 1-2-3 corrects the
word and continues
checking for spelling
errors.

◆ This area displays
the next word 1-2-3
does not recognize.

Skip misspelled word

6 If you do not want to change
the spelling of the word, move
the mouse ₖ over **Skip** and then
press the left button.

◆ Correct or skip spelling errors
until 1-2-3 finishes checking
your worksheet.

49

Overview

USING FORMULAS AND FUNCTIONS

Formulas

Enter a Formula

Functions

Enter a Function

Add Numbers

Errors in Formulas

Copy Formulas

Name Cells

◆ In this chapter you will learn how to enter formulas and functions into your worksheet. This lets you perform calculations on your worksheet data.

FORMULAS

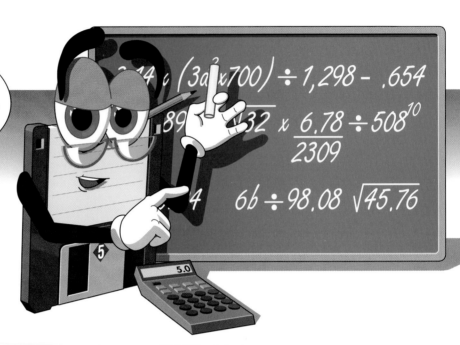

You can use formulas to perform calculations on your worksheet data.

INTRODUCTION TO FORMULAS

◆ You must begin a formula with a plus sign (**+**).

◆ You should use cell addresses (example: **A1**) instead of actual numbers whenever possible. This way, if your data changes, 1-2-3 will automatically redo the calculations.

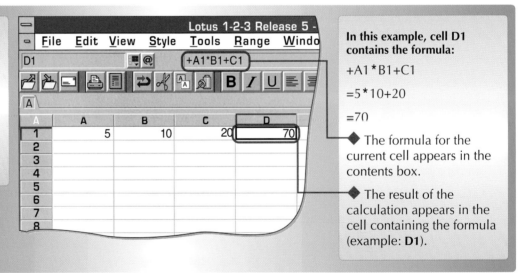

In this example, cell **D1** contains the formula:

$$+A1*B1+C1$$

$$=5*10+20$$

$$=70$$

◆ The formula for the current cell appears in the contents box.

◆ The result of the calculation appears in the cell containing the formula (example: **D1**).

Getting Started	Save and Open Your Files	Edit Your Worksheets	**Using Formulas and Functions**	Working with Rows and Columns	Format Your Worksheets	Print Your Worksheets

Using Formulas and Functions

- **Formulas**
- Enter a Formula
- Functions
- Enter a Function

- Add Numbers
- Errors in Formulas
- Copy Formulas
- Name Cells

You can use these operators in your formulas:

+	Addition
-	Subtraction
*	Multiplication
/	Division
^	Exponentiation

1-2-3 will perform calculations in the following order:

1 Exponentiation

2 Multiplication and Division

3 Addition and Subtraction

You can change the order that 1-2-3 calculates your formulas by using parentheses ( ).

◆ 1-2-3 will calculate the numbers in parentheses first.

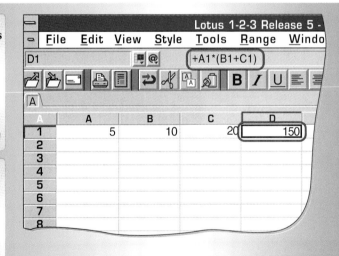

In this example, cell D1 contains the formula:

+A1*(B1+C1)

=5*(10+20)

=150

ENTER A FORMULA

You can enter a formula into any cell in your worksheet.

ENTER A FORMULA

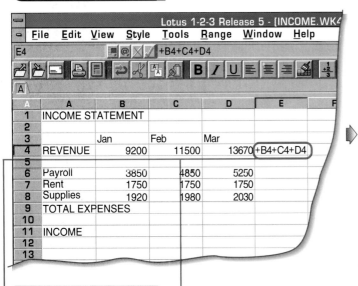

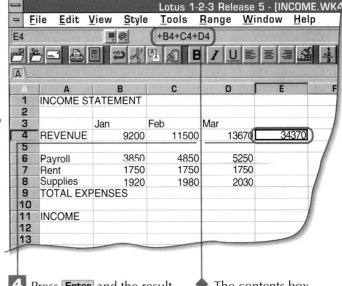

1 Move the mouse ⌖ over the cell where you want to enter a formula and then press the left button.

2 Type a plus sign (+) to begin the formula.

3 Type the calculation you want to perform (example: **B4+C4+D4**).

Note: This formula will calculate the total Revenue.

4 Press **Enter** and the result of the calculation appears in the cell (example: **34370**).

◆ The contents box displays the formula for the current cell.

Getting Started	Save and Open Your Files	Edit Your Worksheets	**Using Formulas and Functions**	Working with Rows and Columns	Format Your Worksheets	Print Your Worksheets

- Formulas
- **Enter a Formula**
- Functions
- Enter a Function

- Add Numbers
- Errors in Formulas
- Copy Formulas
- Name Cells

Tip

ERR

◆ If **ERR** appears in a cell, 1-2-3 cannot properly calculate the formula you entered.

Note: For more information on errors in formulas, refer to page 62.

AUTOMATIC RECALCULATION

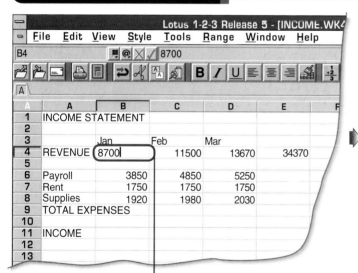

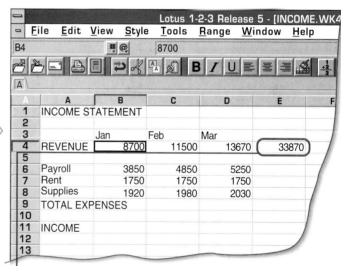

If you change a number used in a formula, 1-2-3 will automatically calculate a new result.

1 Move the mouse ⌖ over the cell you want to change (example: **B4**) and then press the left button.

2 Type a new number (example: **8700**).

3 Press `Enter` and 1-2-3 automatically recalculates the formula using the new number.

FUNCTIONS

A function is a ready-to-use formula. 1-2-3 offers over 200 functions to perform specialized calculations on your worksheet data.

INTRODUCTION TO FUNCTIONS

You must tell 1-2-3 which data you want to use to calculate a function. The data is enclosed in parentheses ( ).

@SUM(A1,A3,A5)

◆ When there is a comma (,) between cell addresses in a function, 1-2-3 uses each cell to perform the calculation.

Example: @SUM(A1,A3,A5) is the same as the formula +A1+A3+A5.

@SUM(A1..A4)

◆ When there are two periods (..) between cell addresses in a function, 1-2-3 uses the displayed cells and all cells between them to perform the calculation.

Example: @SUM(A1..A4) is the same as the formula +A1+A2+A3+A4.

| Getting Started | Save and Open Your Files | Edit Your Worksheets | Using Formulas and Functions | Working with Rows and Columns | Format Your Worksheets | Print Your Worksheets |

- Formulas
- Enter a Formula
- **Functions**
- Enter a Function

- Add Numbers
- Errors in Formulas
- Copy Formulas
- Name Cells

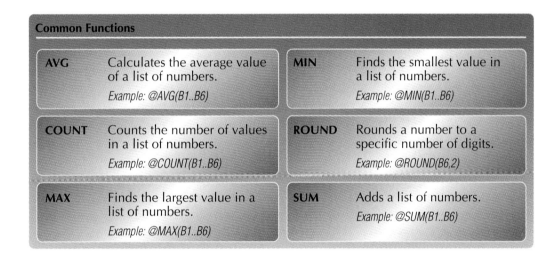

Common Functions

AVG	Calculates the average value of a list of numbers. *Example: @AVG(B1..B6)*	**MIN**	Finds the smallest value in a list of numbers. *Example: @MIN(B1..B6)*
COUNT	Counts the number of values in a list of numbers. *Example: @COUNT(B1..B6)*	**ROUND**	Rounds a number to a specific number of digits. *Example: @ROUND(B6,2)*
MAX	Finds the largest value in a list of numbers. *Example: @MAX(B1..B6)*	**SUM**	Adds a list of numbers. *Example: @SUM(B1..B6)*

◆ A function starts with the @ symbol.

◆ You should use cell addresses (example: **A1**) instead of actual numbers whenever possible. This way, if your data changes, 1-2-3 will automatically redo the calculations.

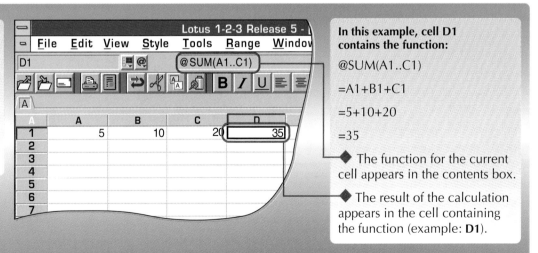

In this example, cell D1 contains the function:

@SUM(A1..C1)

=A1+B1+C1

=5+10+20

=35

◆ The function for the current cell appears in the contents box.

◆ The result of the calculation appears in the cell containing the function (example: **D1**).

ENTER A FUNCTION

Functions let you perform specialized calculations without typing complex formulas.

ENTER A FUNCTION

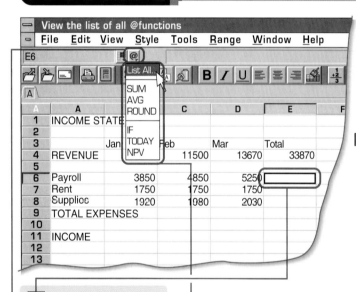

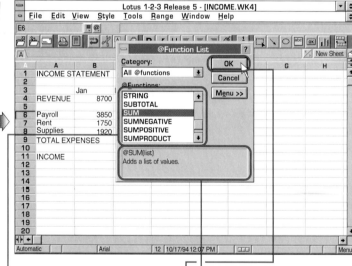

1 Move the mouse ▷ over the cell where you want to enter a function and then press the left button.

2 To display a list of frequently used functions, move the mouse ▷ over @ and then press the left button.

Note: If the function you want to use appears in this list, move the mouse ▷ over the function and then press the left button. Then skip to step **6***.*

3 To display a list of all the functions, move the mouse ▷ over **List All** and then press the left button.

◆ The **@Function List** dialog box appears.

4 Move the mouse ▷ over the function you want to use (example: **SUM**) and then press the left button.

Note: To view all of the available functions, use the scroll bar. For more information, refer to page 21.

◆ This area displays a description of the function you selected.

5 Move the mouse ▷ over **OK** and then press the left button.

| Getting Started | Save and Open Your Files | Edit Your Worksheets | Using Formulas and Functions | Working with Rows and Columns | Format Your Worksheets | Print Your Worksheets |

- Formulas
- Enter a Formula
- Functions
- **Enter a Function**

- Add Numbers
- Errors in Formulas
- Copy Formulas
- Name Cells

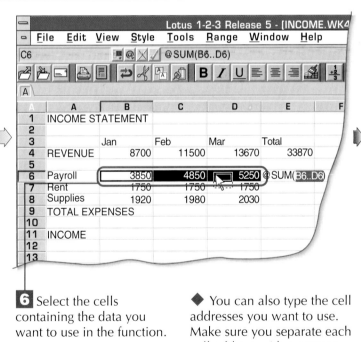

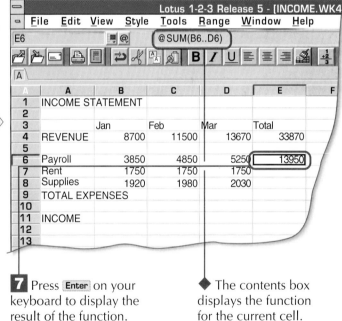

6 Select the cells containing the data you want to use in the function.

Note: To select cells, refer to page 14.

◆ You can also type the cell addresses you want to use. Make sure you separate each cell address with a comma (example: **B6,C6,D6**).

7 Press Enter on your keyboard to display the result of the function.

◆ The contents box displays the function for the current cell.

ADD NUMBERS

You can use the Sum SmartIcon to quickly add a list of numbers in your worksheet.

ADD A LIST OF NUMBERS

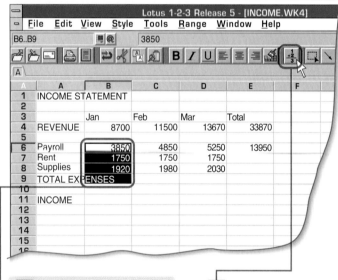

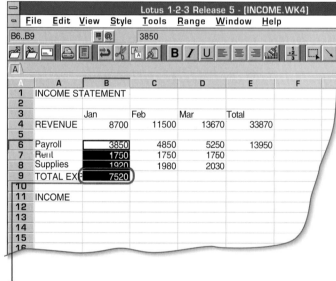

1 Select the cells containing the numbers you want to sum, including a blank cell for the result.

Note: To select cells, refer to page 14.

2 Move the mouse over ⅓ and then press the left button.

◆ The result appears.

| Getting Started | Save and Open Your Files | Edit Your Worksheets | **Using Formulas and Functions** | Working with Rows and Columns | Format Your Worksheets | Print Your Worksheets |

- Formulas
- Enter a Formula
- Functions
- Enter a Function

- **Add Numbers**
- Errors in Formulas
- Copy Formulas
- Name Cells

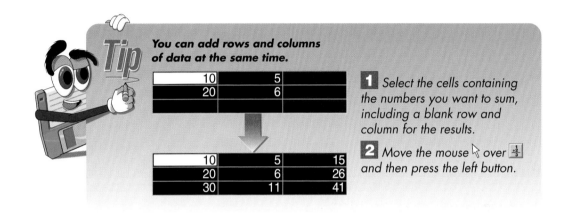

Tip

You can add rows and columns of data at the same time.

10	5	
20	6	

10	5	15
20	6	26
30	11	41

1 Select the cells containing the numbers you want to sum, including a blank row and column for the results.

2 Move the mouse ⬚ over 🔢 and then press the left button.

ADD SEVERAL LISTS OF NUMBERS

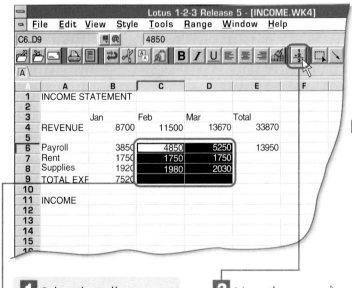

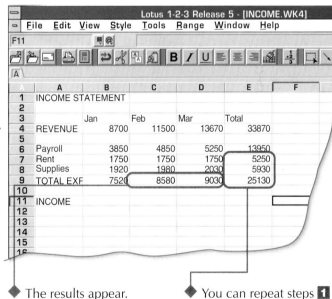

1 Select the cells containing the numbers you want to sum, including blank cells for the results.

Note: To select cells, refer to page 14.

2 Move the mouse ⬚ over 🔢 and then press the left button.

◆ The results appear.

◆ You can repeat steps **1** and **2** to add other lists of numbers in your worksheet.

Note: To deselect cells, move the mouse ⬚ outside the selected area and then press the left button.

ERRORS IN FORMULAS

An error message appears when 1-2-3 cannot properly calculate a formula. You can correct an error by editing the cell displaying the error message.

COMMON ERRORS IN FORMULAS

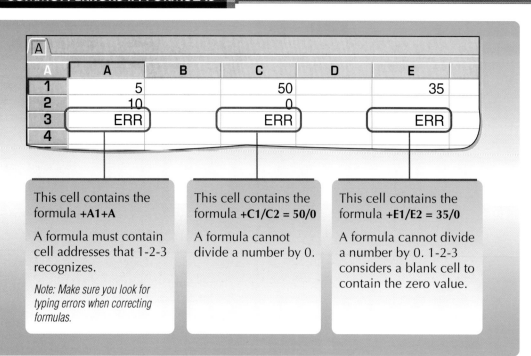

This cell contains the formula **+A1+A**

A formula must contain cell addresses that 1-2-3 recognizes.

Note: Make sure you look for typing errors when correcting formulas.

This cell contains the formula **+C1/C2 = 50/0**

A formula cannot divide a number by 0.

This cell contains the formula **+E1/E2 = 35/0**

A formula cannot divide a number by 0. 1-2-3 considers a blank cell to contain the zero value.

CORRECT AN ERROR

1 To correct an error, move the mouse ⬚ over the cell displaying the error message and then quickly press the left button twice.

2 Edit the formula as you would any data in your worksheet.

Note: To edit data, refer to page 40.

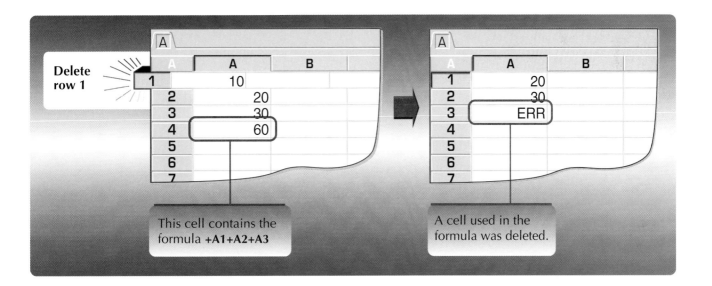

Delete row 1

This cell contains the formula +A1+A2+A3

A cell used in the formula was deleted.

COPY FORMULAS

After entering a formula in your worksheet, you can copy the formula to other cells. This saves you time when entering the same formula into several cells.

COPY FORMULAS (USING RELATIVE REFERENCES)

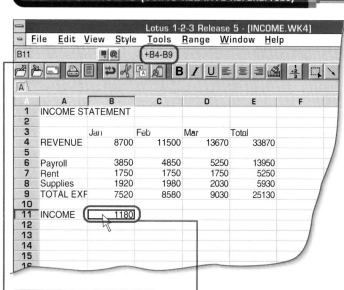

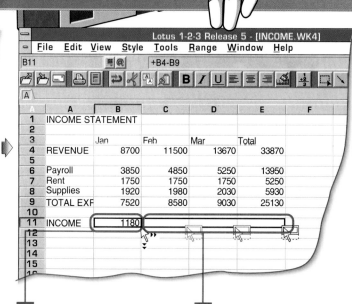

1 Enter the formula you want to copy to other cells (example: to calculate INCOME, enter **+B4-B9** in cell **B11**).

2 Move the mouse ⬚ over the cell containing the formula and then press the left button.

3 Move the mouse ⬚ over the bottom right corner of the cell and ⬚ changes to ⬚".

4 Press and hold down the left button as you drag the mouse ⬚ over the cells you want to receive a copy of the formula.

Getting Started	Save and Open Your Files	Edit Your Worksheets	Using Formulas and Functions	Working with Rows and Columns	Format Your Worksheets	Print Your Worksheets

- Formulas
- Enter a Formula
- Functions
- Enter a Function

- Add Numbers
- Errors in Formulas
- **Copy Formulas**
- Name Cells

When you copy a formula, 1-2-3 automatically changes the cell addresses in the new formulas.

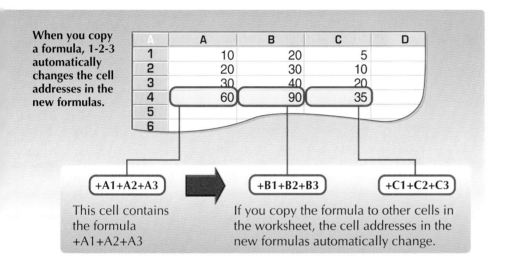

+A1+A2+A3

This cell contains the formula +A1+A2+A3

+B1+B2+B3   **+C1+C2+C3**

If you copy the formula to other cells in the worksheet, the cell addresses in the new formulas automatically change.

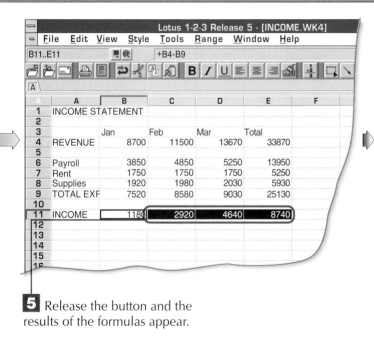

5 Release the button and the results of the formulas appear.

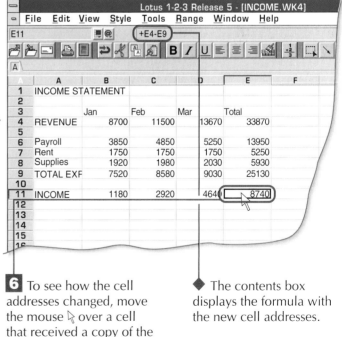

6 To see how the cell addresses changed, move the mouse ⬚ over a cell that received a copy of the formula (example: **E11**) and then press the left button.

◆ The contents box displays the formula with the new cell addresses.

65

COPY FORMULAS

To save time, you can copy a formula to other cells in your worksheet. If you do not want 1-2-3 to change a cell address when copying the formula, you must lock the cell. A locked cell address is called an absolute reference.

COPY FORMULAS (USING ABSOLUTE REFERENCES)

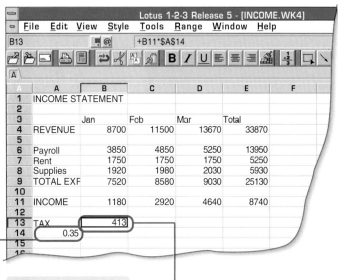

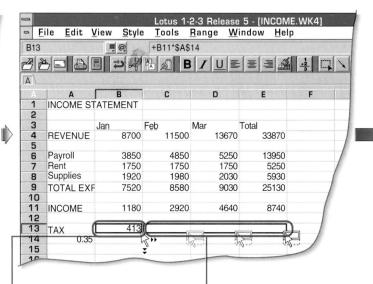

1 Enter the data you want to use as an absolute cell reference (example: **0.35** in cell **A14**).

2 Enter the formula you want to copy to other cells (example: to calculate TAX, enter **+B11*$A$14** in cell **B13**).

Note: To lock a cell address during the copy process, type a dollar sign ($) before both the column letter and row number (example: $A$14).

3 Move the mouse ⍟ over the cell containing the formula you want to copy (example: **B13**) and then press the left button.

4 Move the mouse ⍟ over the bottom right corner of the cell and ⍟ changes to ⍟.

5 Press and hold down the left button as you drag the mouse ⍟ over the cells you want to receive a copy of the formula.

INTRODUCTION TO LOTUS 1-2-3

| Getting Started | Save and Open Your Files | Edit Your Worksheets | **Using Formulas and Functions** | Working with Rows and Columns | Format Your Worksheets | Print Your Worksheets |

- Formulas
- Enter a Formula
- Functions
- Enter a Function

- Add Numbers
- Errors in Formulas
- **Copy Formulas**
- Name Cells

To make a cell reference absolute, type a dollar sign ($) before both the column letter and row number (example: $B$1).

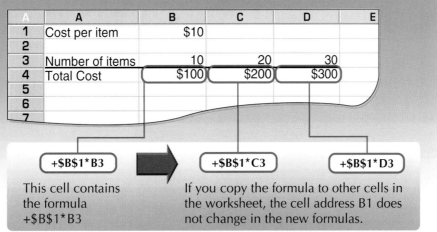

A	A	B	C	D	E
1	Cost per item	$10			
2					
3	Number of items	10	20	30	
4	Total Cost	$100	$200	$300	
5					
6					
7					

+$B$1*B3 → +$B$1*C3   +$B$1*D3

This cell contains the formula +$B$1*B3

If you copy the formula to other cells in the worksheet, the cell address B1 does not change in the new formulas.

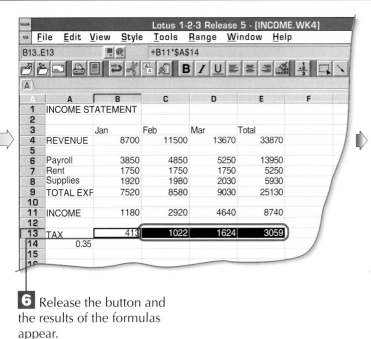

6 Release the button and the results of the formulas appear.

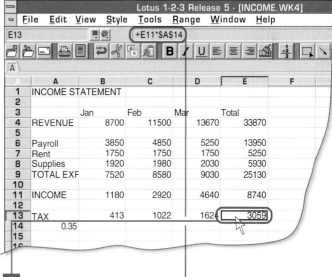

7 To see how the cell addresses changed, move the mouse over a cell that received a copy of the formula (example: **E13**) and then press the left button.

◆ The absolute reference in the formula did not change (example: **A14**). The relative reference in the formula did change (example: **E11**).

NAME CELLS

You can use names to refer to cells in your worksheet. This saves you time when selecting cells or entering formulas.

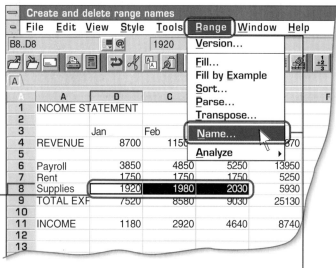

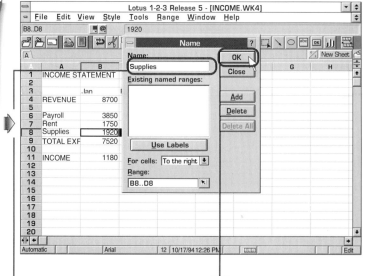

1 Select the cells you want to name.

Note: To select cells, refer to page 14.

2 Move the mouse ☐ over **Range** and then press the left button.

3 Move the mouse ☐ over **Name** and then press the left button.

◆ The **Name** dialog box appears.

4 Type a name for the cells (example: **Supplies**).

5 Move the mouse ☐ over **OK** and then press the left button.

Note: To deselect the cells, move the mouse ☐ over any cell in the worksheet and then press the left button.

Getting Started	Save and Open Your Files	Edit Your Worksheets	Using Formulas and Functions	Working with Rows and Columns	Format Your Worksheets	Print Your Worksheets

- Formulas
- Enter a Formula
- Functions
- Enter a Function

- Add Numbers
- Errors in Formulas
- Copy Formulas
- **Name Cells**

Named cells make formulas and functions easier to enter and understand.

A	A	B	C
1		**Pens Sold**	
2	Jan	$500	
3	Feb	$800	
4	Mar	$1,000	
5	Apr	$700	
6	Total	$3,000	
7			

◆ This group of cells (B2 to B5) is named PENS.

◆ This cell contains the function @SUM(PENS).

@SUM(PENS) is easier to enter and understand than the function @SUM(B2..B5) because it contains a name instead of cell addresses.

SELECT NAMED CELLS

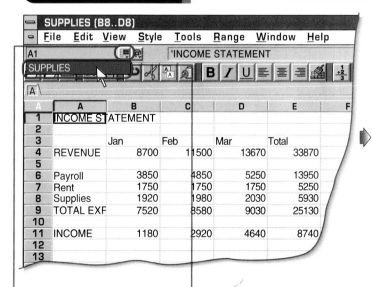

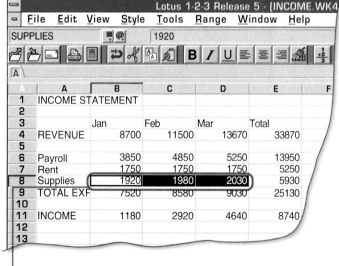

After you name cells in your worksheet, you can quickly select the cells.

1 Move the mouse ⍼ over 🖳 and then press the left button.

2 Move the mouse ⍼ over the name of the cells you want to select and then press the left button.

◆ The cells are selected.

verview

WORKING WITH ROWS AND COLUMNS

Insert a Row or Column

Delete a Row or Column

Change Column Width

Change Row Height

Hide Columns

◆ In this chapter you will learn how to add, delete and adjust rows and columns in your worksheet.

INSERT A ROW
OR COLUMN

You can add a row or column to your worksheet if you want to insert new data.

INSERT A ROW

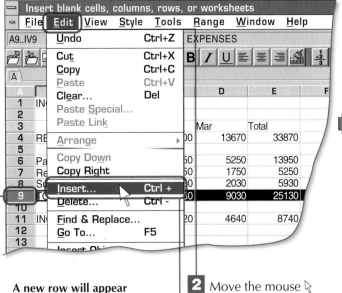

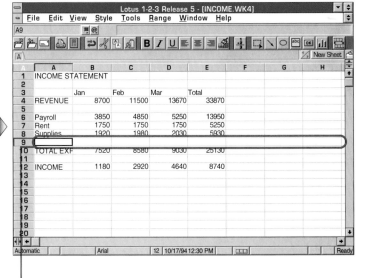

A new row will appear above the row you select.

1 To select a row, move the mouse ⇗ over the row heading (example: **row 9**) and then press the left button.

2 Move the mouse ⇗ over **Edit** and then press the left button.

3 Move the mouse ⇗ over **Insert** and then press the left button.

◆ The new row appears and all the rows that follow shift downward.

Getting Started	Save and Open Your Files	Edit Your Worksheets	Using Formulas and Functions	**Working with Rows and Columns**	Format Your Worksheets	Print Your Worksheets

- **Insert a Row or Column**
- Delete a Row or Column
- Change Column Width
- Change Row Height
- Hide Columns

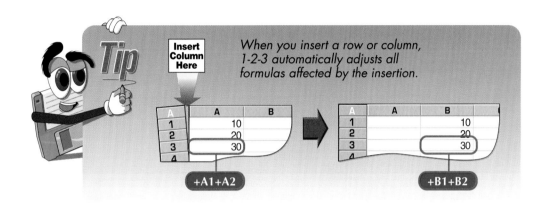

Tip

Insert Column Here

When you insert a row or column, 1-2-3 automatically adjusts all formulas affected by the insertion.

+A1+A2 → +B1+B2

INSERT A COLUMN

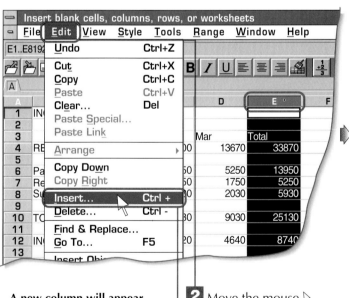

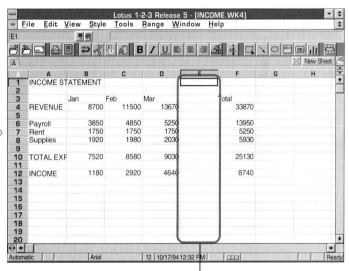

A new column will appear to the left of the column you select.

1 To select a column, move the mouse over the column heading (example: **column E**) and then press the left button.

2 Move the mouse over **Edit** and then press the left button.

3 Move the mouse over **Insert** and then press the left button.

◆ The new column appears and all the columns that follow shift to the right.

DELETE A ROW OR COLUMN

You can delete a row or column from your worksheet. This lets you remove cells you no longer need.

DELETE A ROW

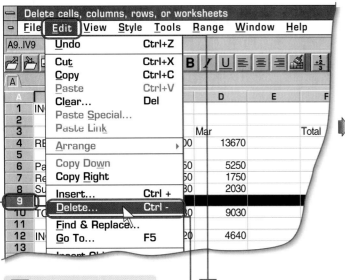

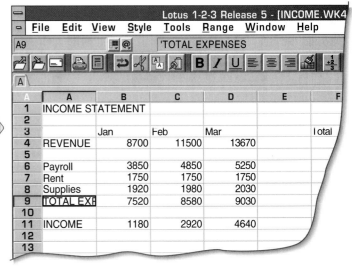

1 To select the row you want to delete, move the mouse over the row heading (example: **row 9**) and then press the left button.

2 Move the mouse over **Edit** and then press the left button.

3 Move the mouse over **Delete** and then press the left button.

◆ The row disappears and all the rows that follow shift upward.

| Getting Started | Save and Open Your Files | Edit Your Worksheets | Using Formulas and Functions | **Working with Rows and Columns** | Format Your Worksheets | Print Your Worksheets |

- Insert a Row or Column
- **Delete a Row or Column**
- Change Column Width
- Change Row Height
- Hide Columns

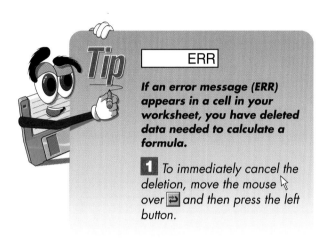

Tip

ERR

If an error message (ERR) appears in a cell in your worksheet, you have deleted data needed to calculate a formula.

1 *To immediately cancel the deletion, move the mouse over ⏎ and then press the left button.*

DELETE A COLUMN

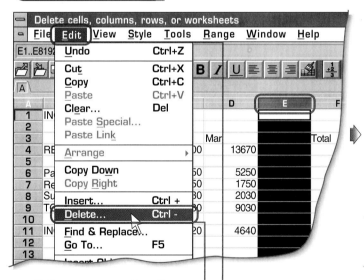

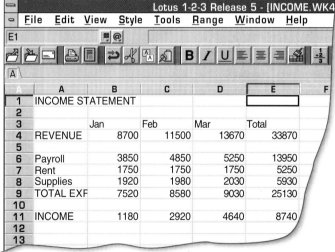

1 To select the column you want to delete, move the mouse ⇧ over the column heading (example: **column E**) and then press the left button.

2 Move the mouse ⇧ over **Edit** and then press the left button.

3 Move the mouse ⇧ over **Delete** and then press the left button.

◆ The column disappears and all the columns that follow shift to the left.

CHANGE COLUMN WIDTH

> You can improve the appearance of your worksheet and display hidden data by changing the width of columns.

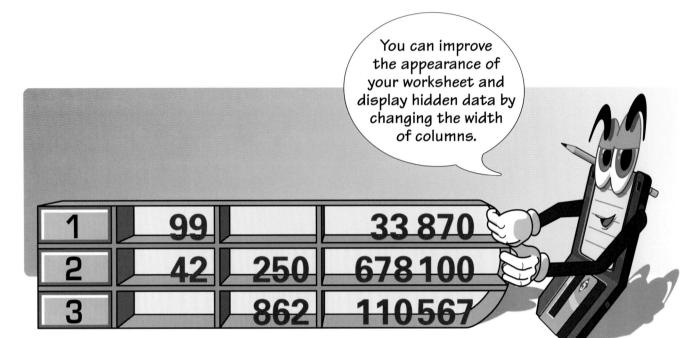

CHANGE COLUMN WIDTH

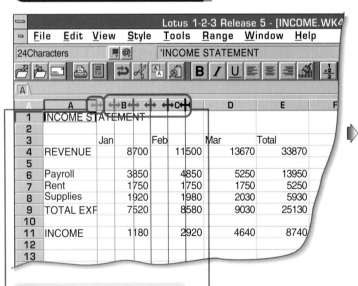

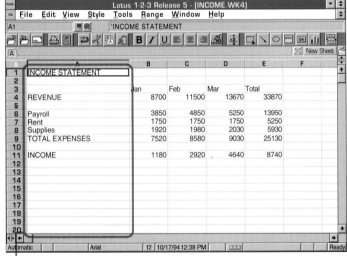

1 Move the mouse ⌖ over the right edge of the column heading you want to change (example: **column A**) and ⌖ changes to **+**.

2 Press and hold down the left button as you drag the edge of the column to a new position.

◆ A line indicates the new column width.

3 Release the button and the new column width appears.

Getting Started	Save and Open Your Files	Edit Your Worksheets	Using Formulas and Functions	**Working with Rows and Columns**	Format Your Worksheets	Print Your Worksheets

Working with Rows and Columns

- Insert a Row or Column
- Delete a Row or Column
- **Change Column Width**
- Change Row Height
- Hide Columns

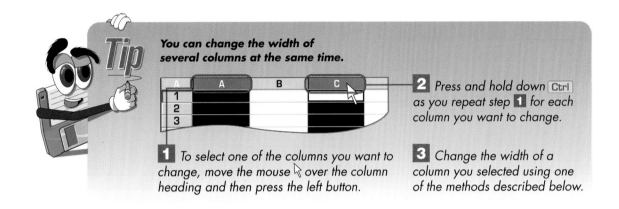

Tip

You can change the width of several columns at the same time.

2 Press and hold down `Ctrl` as you repeat step **1** for each column you want to change.

1 To select one of the columns you want to change, move the mouse ⇖ over the column heading and then press the left button.

3 Change the width of a column you selected using one of the methods described below.

CHANGE COLUMN WIDTH AUTOMATICALLY

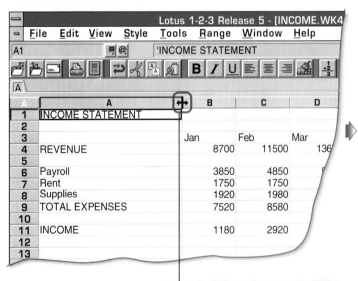

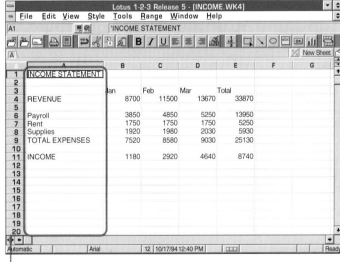

You can have 1-2-3 adjust a column width to fit the longest item in the column.

1 Move the mouse ⇖ over the right edge of the column heading you want to change (example: **column A**) and ⇖ changes to **+**.

2 Quickly press the left button twice.

◆ The column width changes to fit the longest item in the column.

CHANGE ROW HEIGHT

You can change the height of a row. This is useful if you want to add space between the rows of data in your worksheet.

CHANGE ROW HEIGHT

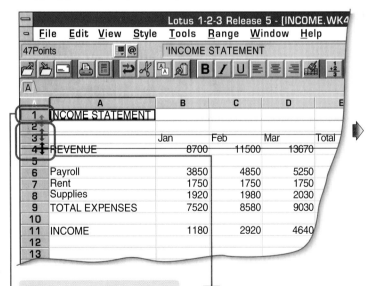

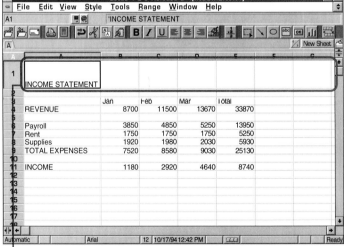

1 Move the mouse ⌖ over the bottom edge of the row heading you want to change (example: **row 1**) and ⌖ changes to ✛.

2 Press and hold down the left button as you drag the edge of the row to a new position.

◆ A line indicates the new row height.

3 Release the button and the new row height appears.

Getting Started	Save and Open Your Files	Edit Your Worksheets	Using Formulas and Functions	Working with Rows and Columns	Format Your Worksheets	Print Your Worksheets

Working with Rows and Columns

• Insert a Row or Column
• Delete a Row or Column
• Change Column Width
• **Change Row Height**
• Hide Columns

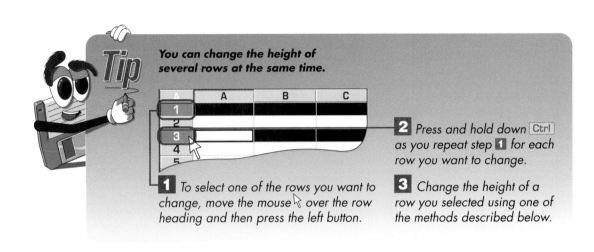

Tip

You can change the height of several rows at the same time.

1 To select one of the rows you want to change, move the mouse ⇳ over the row heading and then press the left button.

2 Press and hold down `Ctrl` as you repeat step **1** for each row you want to change.

3 Change the height of a row you selected using one of the methods described below.

CHANGE ROW HEIGHT AUTOMATICALLY

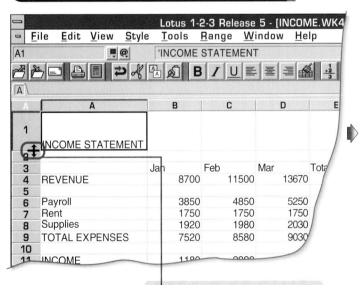

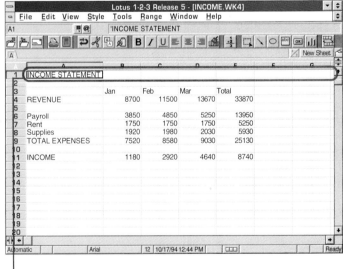

You can have 1-2-3 adjust a row height to fit the tallest item in the row.

1 Move the mouse ⇳ over the bottom edge of the row heading you want to change (example: **row 1**) and ⇳ changes to ✚ .

2 Quickly press the left button twice.

◆ The row height changes to fit the tallest item in the row.

79

HIDE COLUMNS

> If you do not want other people to view confidential information in your worksheet, you can hide the columns containing the data.

Hide

- ● **Column**
- ○ **Sheet**

Range:

`B4..D4`

OK

Cancel

Show

HIDE COLUMNS

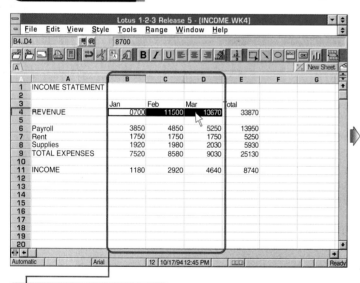

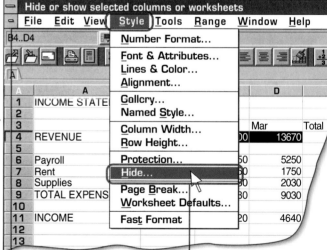

1 Select one cell in each column you want to hide.

Note: To select cells, refer to page 14.

2 Move the mouse ⤵ over **Style** and then press the left button.

3 Move the mouse ⤵ over **Hide** and then press the left button.

INTRODUCTION TO LOTUS 1-2-3

| Getting Started | Save and Open Your Files | Edit Your Worksheets | Using Formulas and Functions | **Working with Rows and Columns** | Format Your Worksheets | Print Your Worksheets |

- Insert a Row or Column
- Delete a Row or Column
- Change Column Width
- Change Row Height
- **Hide Columns**

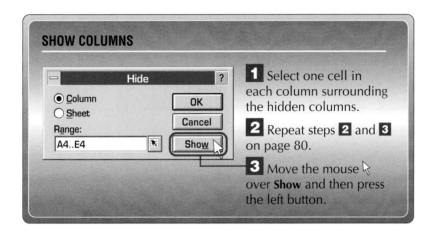

SHOW COLUMNS

1 Select one cell in each column surrounding the hidden columns.

2 Repeat steps **2** and **3** on page 80.

3 Move the mouse over **Show** and then press the left button.

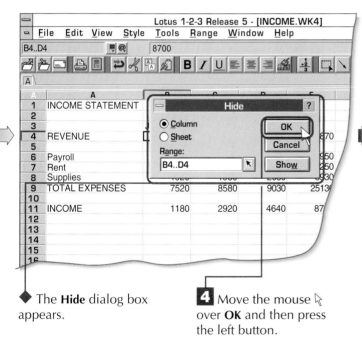

◆ The **Hide** dialog box appears.

4 Move the mouse over **OK** and then press the left button.

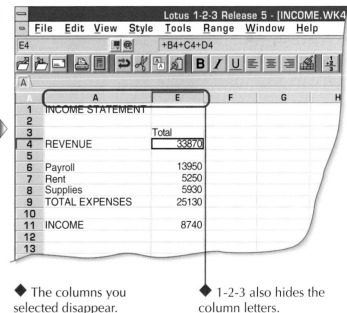

◆ The columns you selected disappear.

Note: The hidden columns will not appear when you print the worksheet. To print a worksheet, refer to page 110.

◆ 1-2-3 also hides the column letters.

81

verview

FORMAT YOUR WORKSHEETS

Change Appearance of Numbers

Bold, Italic and Underline

Align Data

Change Fonts

Center Data Across Columns

Add Borders

Add Color or Shading

Clear Styles

Copy Styles

Style Data Automatically

◆ In this chapter you will learn how to change the appearance of data in your worksheet.

CHANGE APPEARANCE OF NUMBERS

You can change the appearance of numbers in your worksheet without retyping them. This can make the numbers easier to understand.

Number Style	Example
Scientific	1.04E+03
Comma	1,038.00
Percent	103800.00%
US Dollar	$1,038.00
Japanese Yen	¥1,038

CHANGE APPEARANCE OF NUMBERS

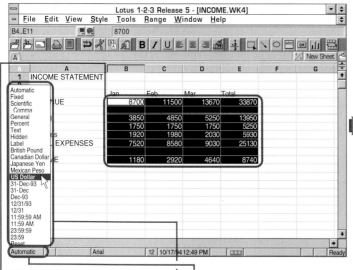

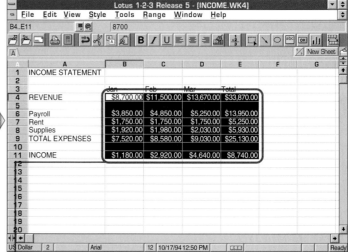

1 Select the cells containing the numbers you want to change.

Note: To select cells, refer to page 14.

2 Move the mouse ⤣ over this box and then press the left button.

3 Move the mouse ⤣ over the style you want to use (example: **US Dollar**) and then press the left button.

◆ The numbers in the cells you selected display the new style.

INTRODUCTION TO LOTUS 1-2-3

| Getting Started | Save and Open Your Files | Edit Your Worksheets | Using Formulas and Functions | Working with Rows and Columns | **Format Your Worksheets** | Print Your Worksheets |

- • **Change Appearance of Numbers**
- • Bold, Italic and Underline
- • Align Data
- • Change Fonts
- • Center Data Across Columns
- • Add Borders
- • Add Color or Shading
- • Clear Styles
- • Copy Styles
- • Style Data Automatically

Tip

If asterisks (*) appear in a cell, the column is not wide enough to display the entire number.

****

Note: To change the column width, refer to page 76.

CHANGE NUMBER OF DECIMAL PLACES

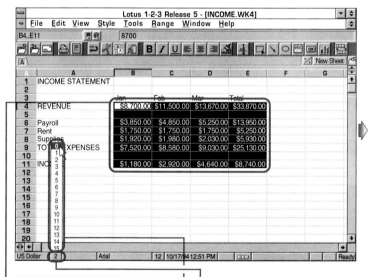

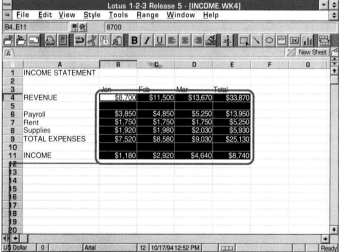

1 Select the cells containing the numbers you want to change.

Note: To select cells, refer to page 14.

2 Move the mouse ⌖ over this box and then press the left button.

3 Move the mouse ⌖ over the number of decimal places you want to display (example: **0**) and then press the left button.

◆ The numbers in the cells you selected display the new number of decimal places.

85

BOLD, ITALIC AND UNDERLINE   ALIGN DATA

You can use the Bold, Italic and Underline features to emphasize important data.

bold   *italic*   underline

BOLD, ITALIC AND UNDERLINE

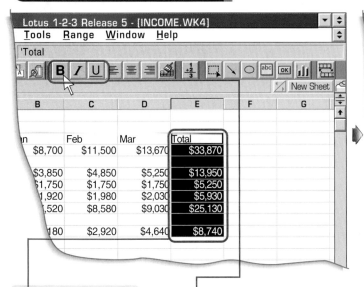

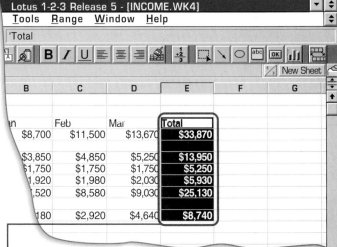

1 Select the cells containing the data you want to change.

Note: To select cells, refer to page 14.

2 Move the mouse ⇧ over one of the following options and then press the left button.

B	Bold data
I	Italicize data
U	Underline data

◆ The data in the cells you selected appears in the new style.

Note: In this example, the data appears in the bold style.

Remove Bold, Italic or Underline

Repeat steps **1** and **2**.

| Getting Started | Save and Open Your Files | Edit Your Worksheets | Using Formulas and Functions | Working with Rows and Columns | **Format Your Worksheets** | Print Your Worksheets |

- Change Appearance of Numbers
- **Bold, Italic and Underline**
- **Align Data**
- Change Fonts
- Center Data Across Columns

- Add Borders
- Add Color or Shading
- Clear Styles
- Copy Styles
- Style Data Automatically

You can change the position of data in each cell of your worksheet. 1-2-3 offers several alignment options.

ALIGN DATA

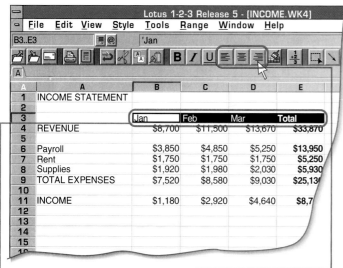

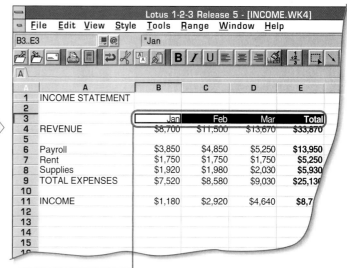

1 Select the cells containing the data you want to align.

Note: To select cells, refer to page 14.

2 Move the mouse ▷ over one of the following options and then press the left button.

≣ Left-align data

≣ Center data

≣ Right-align data

◆ The data in the cells you selected displays the new alignment.

Note: In this example, the data appears right-aligned in the cells.

CHANGE FONTS

You can change the design of data to give your worksheet a new look.

CHANGE TYPEFACE

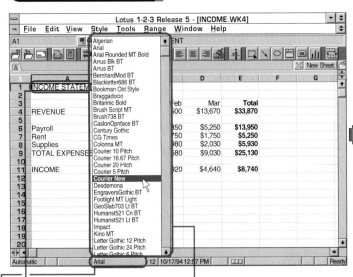

1 Select the cell(s) containing the data you want to change to a new typeface (example: **A1**).

2 Move the mouse ⌖ over this box and then press the left button.

3 Move the mouse ⌖ over the typeface you want to use (example: **Courier New**) and then press the left button.

Note: To view all of the available typefaces, use the scroll bar. For more information, refer to page 21.

◆ The data in the cell(s) you selected changes to the new typeface.

Getting Started	Save and Open Your Files	Edit Your Worksheets	Using Formulas and Functions	Working with Rows and Columns	**Format Your Worksheets**	Print Your Worksheets

- Change Appearance of Numbers
- Bold, Italic and Underline
- Align Data
- **Change Fonts**
- Center Data Across Columns
- Add Borders
- Add Color or Shading
- Clear Styles
- Copy Styles
- Style Data Automatically

You can change the size of data in your worksheet to make the data easier to read.

6 point

12 point

14 point

18 point

24 point

1-2-3 measures the size of data in points. There are approximately 72 points per inch.

CHANGE FONT SIZE

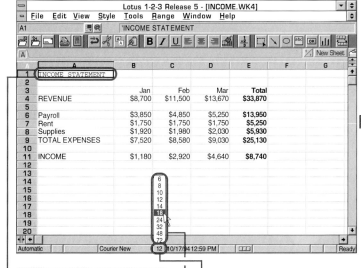

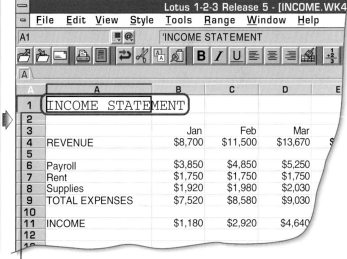

1 Select the cell(s) containing the data you want to change to a new font size.

2 Move the mouse ⬚ over this box and then press the left button.

3 Move the mouse ⬚ over the font size you want to use (example: **18**) and then press the left button.

◆ The data in the cell(s) you selected changes to the new font size.

89

CHANGE FONTS

You can change the design and size of data in your worksheet at the same time by using the Font & Attributes feature.

CHANGE FONTS

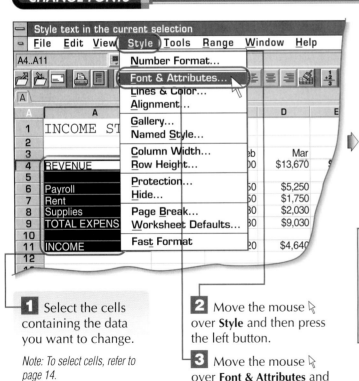

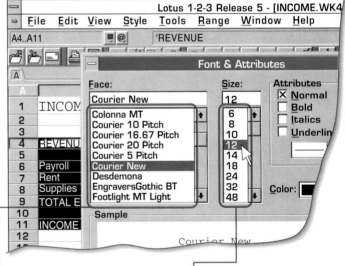

1 Select the cells containing the data you want to change.

Note: To select cells, refer to page 14.

2 Move the mouse ⌖ over **Style** and then press the left button.

3 Move the mouse ⌖ over **Font & Attributes** and then press the left button.

◆ The **Font & Attributes** dialog box appears.

4 Move the mouse ⌖ over the typeface you want to use (example: **Courier New**) and then press the left button.

5 Move the mouse ⌖ over the font size you want to use (example: **12**) and then press the left button.

Note: To view all of the available font options, use the scroll bars. For more information, refer to page 21.

Getting Started	Save and Open Your Files	Edit Your Worksheets	Using Formulas and Functions	Working with Rows and Columns	**Format Your Worksheets**	Print Your Worksheets

- Change Appearance of Numbers
- Bold, Italic and Underline
- Align Data
- **Change Fonts**
- Center Data Across Columns
- Add Borders
- Add Color or Shading
- Clear Styles
- Copy Styles
- Style Data Automatically

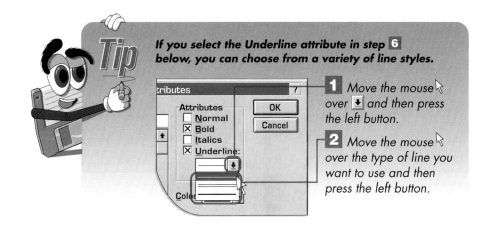

Tip

If you select the Underline attribute in step **6** *below, you can choose from a variety of line styles.*

1 *Move the mouse over* ⬇ *and then press the left button.*

2 *Move the mouse over the type of line you want to use and then press the left button.*

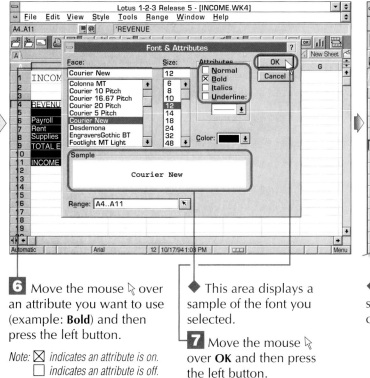

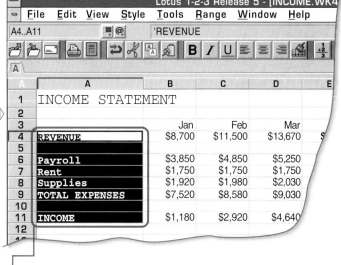

6 Move the mouse ⍴ over an attribute you want to use (example: **Bold**) and then press the left button.

Note: ☒ *indicates an attribute is on.*
☐ *indicates an attribute is off.*

◆ This area displays a sample of the font you selected.

7 Move the mouse ⍴ over **OK** and then press the left button.

◆ The data in the cells you selected displays the font changes.

CENTER DATA ACROSS COLUMNS

You can center data across columns in your worksheet. This is useful for displaying titles.

CENTER DATA ACROSS COLUMNS

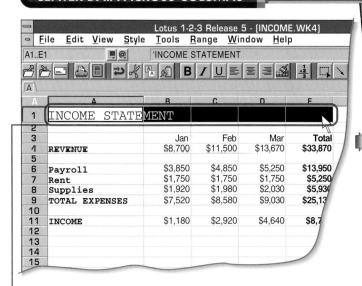

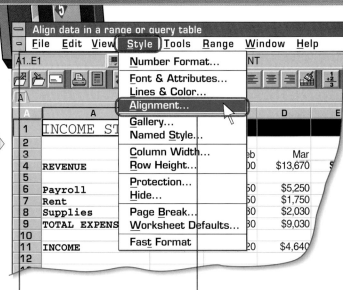

1 To center data across columns, select the cells you want to center the data between.

Note: For best results, the first cell you select should contain the data you want to center.

2 Move the mouse ⟶ over **Style** and then press the left button.

3 Move the mouse ⟶ over **Alignment** and then press the left button.

Getting
Started

Save and
Open Your
Files

Edit Your
Worksheets

Using
Formulas
and Functions

Working with
Rows and
Columns

**Format Your
Worksheets**

Print Your
Worksheets

- Change Appearance of Numbers
- Bold, Italic and Underline
- Align Data
- Change Fonts
- **Center Data Across Columns**

- Add Borders
- Add Color or Shading
- Clear Styles
- Copy Styles
- Style Data Automatically

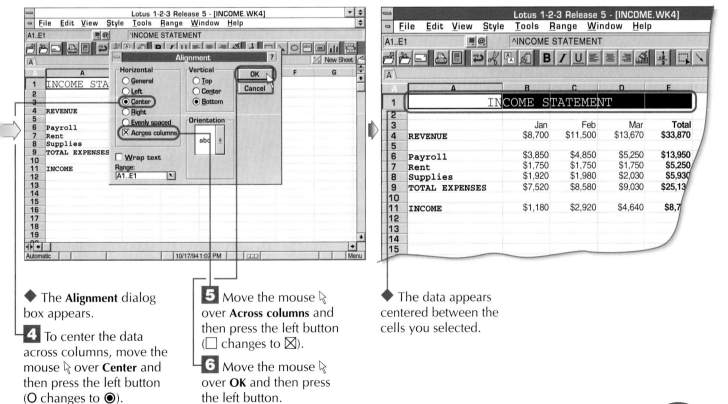

◆ The **Alignment** dialog box appears.

4 To center the data across columns, move the mouse ▷ over **Center** and then press the left button (O changes to ⦿).

5 Move the mouse ▷ over **Across columns** and then press the left button (□ changes to ⊠).

6 Move the mouse ▷ over **OK** and then press the left button.

◆ The data appears centered between the cells you selected.

93

ADD BORDERS

You can add borders to draw attention to important data in your worksheet.

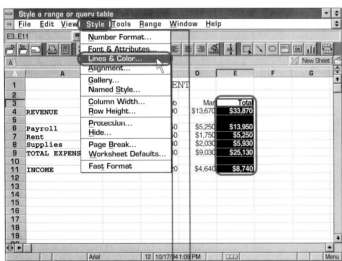

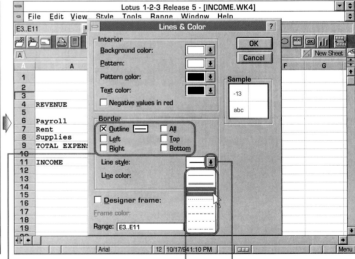

1 Select the cells you want to display borders.

Note: To select cells, refer to page 14.

2 Move the mouse ⬚ over **Style** and then press the left button.

3 Move the mouse ⬚ over **Lines & Color** and then press the left button.

◆ The **Lines & Color** dialog box appears.

4 Move the mouse ⬚ over the border you want to add (example: **Outline**) and then press the left button. □ changes to ⊠.

5 To select a line style for the border, move the mouse ⬚ over ▣ and then press the left button.

6 Move the mouse ⬚ over the line style you want to use and then press the left button.

94

Getting Started	Save and Open Your Files	Edit Your Worksheets	Using Formulas and Functions	Working with Rows and Columns	**Format Your Worksheets**	Print Your Worksheets

- Change Appearance of Numbers
- Bold, Italic and Underline
- Align Data
- Change Fonts
- Center Data Across Columns

- **Add Borders**
- Add Color or Shading
- Clear Styles
- Copy Styles
- Style Data Automatically

Tip

You can use the Gallery feature to have 1-2-3 style your entire worksheet.

Note: For more information, refer to page 102.

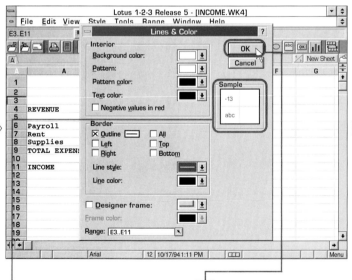

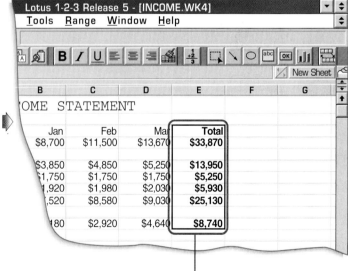

◆ This area displays a sample of the border you selected.

7 Repeat steps **4** to **6** for each border you want to add.

8 Move the mouse ▷ over **OK** and then press the left button.

9 To view the borders, move the mouse ▷ outside the selected area and then press the left button.

◆ The cells display the borders.

ADD COLOR OR SHADING

You can make your worksheet more attractive by adding color or shading.

ADD COLOR OR SHADING

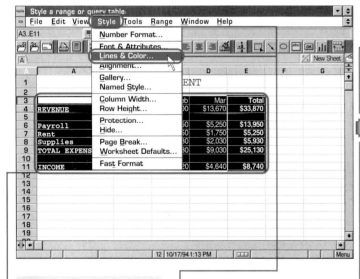

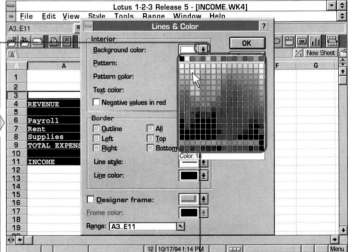

1 Select the cells you want to display color or shading.

Note: To select cells, refer to page 14.

2 Move the mouse ⇗ over **Style** and then press the left button.

3 Move the mouse ⇗ over **Lines & Color** and then press the left button.

◆ The **Lines & Color** dialog box appears.

4 Move the mouse ⇗ over ⬇ beside **Background color:** and then press the left button.

5 Move the mouse ⇗ over the color or shading you want to add and then press the left button.

Getting Started	Save and Open Your Files	Edit Your Worksheets	Using Formulas and Functions	Working with Rows and Columns	**Format Your Worksheets**	Print Your Worksheets

- Change Appearance of Numbers
- Bold, Italic and Underline
- Align Data
- Change Fonts
- Center Data Across Columns

- Add Borders
- **Add Color or Shading**
- Clear Styles
- Copy Styles
- Style Data Automatically

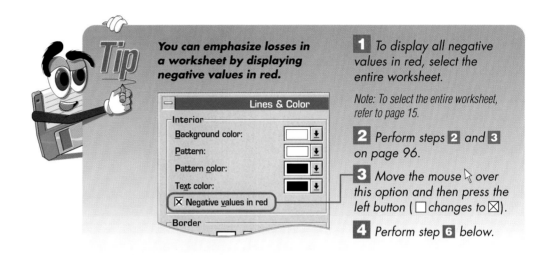

Tip

You can emphasize losses in a worksheet by displaying negative values in red.

1 To display all negative values in red, select the entire worksheet.

Note: To select the entire worksheet, refer to page 15.

2 Perform steps 2 and 3 on page 96.

3 Move the mouse ⇖ over this option and then press the left button (☐ changes to ☒).

4 Perform step 6 below.

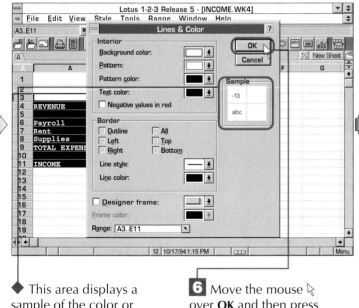

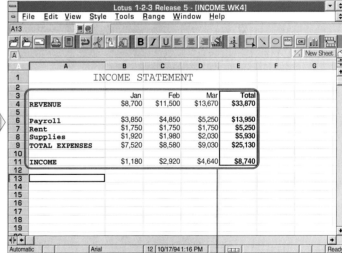

◆ This area displays a sample of the color or shading you selected.

6 Move the mouse ⇖ over **OK** and then press the left button.

7 To view the new color or shading, move the mouse ⇖ outside the selected area and then press the left button.

◆ The cells display the color or shading you selected.

CLEAR STYLES

If you have applied several styles to cells in your worksheet, you can quickly remove all the styles at once.

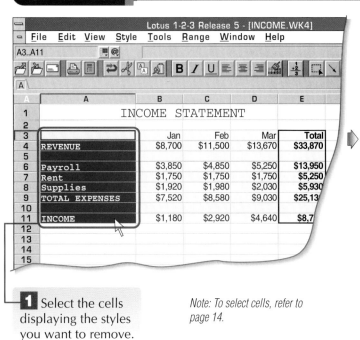

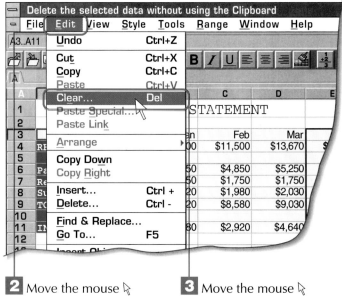

1 Select the cells displaying the styles you want to remove.

Note: To select cells, refer to page 14.

2 Move the mouse � over **Edit** and then press the left button.

3 Move the mouse � over **Clear** and then press the left button.

Getting Started	Save and Open Your Files	Edit Your Worksheets	Using Formulas and Functions	Working with Rows and Columns	Format Your Worksheets	Print Your Worksheets

• Change Appearance of Numbers
• Bold, Italic and Underline
• Align Data
• Change Fonts
• Center Data Across Columns

• Add Borders
• Add Color or Shading
• **Clear Styles**
• Copy Styles
• Style Data Automatically

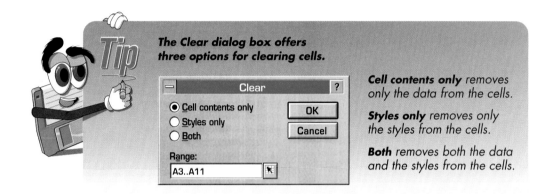

The Clear dialog box offers three options for clearing cells.

Cell contents only *removes only the data from the cells.*

Styles only *removes only the styles from the cells.*

Both *removes both the data and the styles from the cells.*

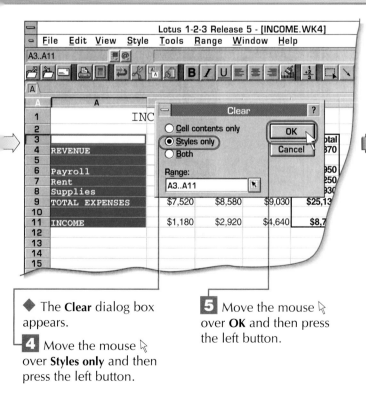

◆ The **Clear** dialog box appears.

4 Move the mouse over **Styles only** and then press the left button.

5 Move the mouse over **OK** and then press the left button.

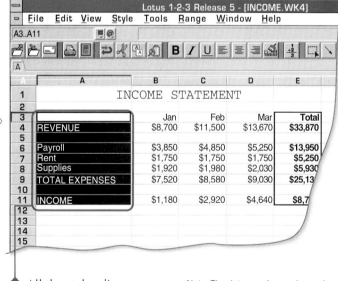

◆ All the styles disappear from the cells you selected.

Note: The data remains unchanged.

COPY STYLES

If you like the appearance of a cell in your worksheet, you can copy the styles to other cells.

style from **CELL B3**

COPY STYLES

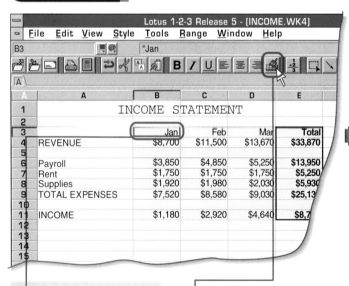

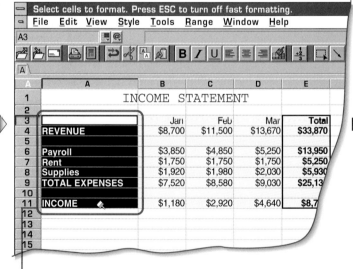

1 Move the mouse ⟍ over the cell displaying the styles you want to copy to other cells and then press the left button.

2 Move the mouse ⟍ over 🖌 and then press the left button.

3 Select the cells you want to look the same.

Note: To select cells, refer to page 14.

INTRODUCTION TO LOTUS 1-2-3

| Getting Started | Save and Open Your Files | Edit Your Worksheets | Using Formulas and Functions | Working with Rows and Columns | **Format Your Worksheets** | Print Your Worksheets |

- Change Appearance of Numbers
- Bold, Italic and Underline
- Align Data
- Change Fonts
- Center Data Across Columns

- Add Borders
- Add Color or Shading
- Clear Styles
- **Copy Styles**
- Style Data Automatically

If the results of the copy are not what you expected, you can immediately cancel the copy using the Undo feature.

1 *Move the mouse ⌖ over ⮌ and then press the left button.*

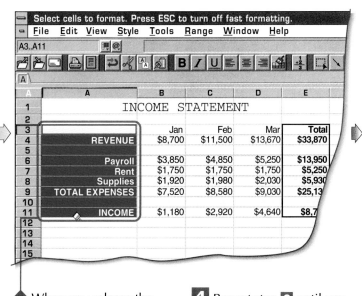

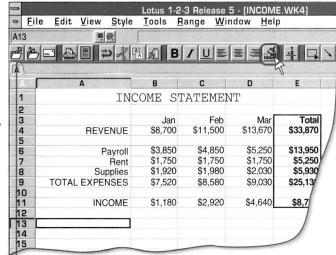

◆ When you release the left button, the cells you selected display the new styles.

4 Repeat step **3** until you have selected all the cells you want to look the same.

5 When you finish copying the styles, move the mouse ⌖ over 🖌 and then press the left button.

Note: You can also press **Esc** *on your keyboard.*

STYLE DATA AUTOMATICALLY

You can quickly change the appearance of data in your worksheet using one of the many designs that 1-2-3 offers.

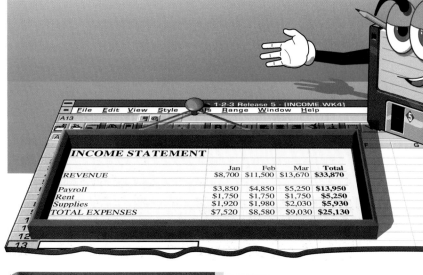

STYLE DATA AUTOMATICALLY

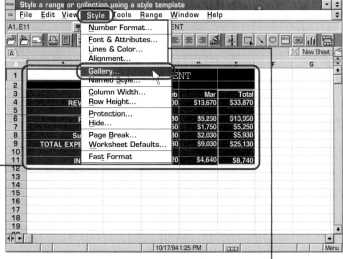

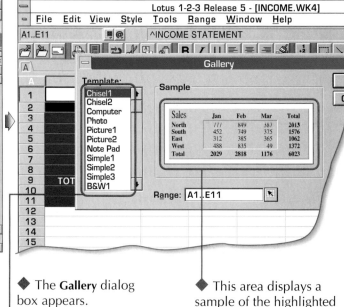

1 Select the cells containing the data you want to style.

Note: To select cells, refer to page 14.

2 Move the mouse ⌖ over **Style** and then press the left button.

3 Move the mouse ⌖ over **Gallery** and then press the left button.

◆ The **Gallery** dialog box appears.

◆ This area displays a list of the available designs.

◆ This area displays a sample of the highlighted design.

| Getting Started | Save and Open Your Files | Edit Your Worksheets | Using Formulas and Functions | Working with Rows and Columns | **Format Your Worksheets** | Print Your Worksheets |

- Change Appearance of Numbers
- Bold, Italic and Underline
- Align Data
- Change Fonts
- Center Data Across Columns

- Add Borders
- Add Color or Shading
- Clear Styles
- Copy Styles
- **Style Data Automatically**

Tip

You can use the **Clear** feature to remove the design you applied to cells in your worksheet.

Note: For more information, refer to page 98.

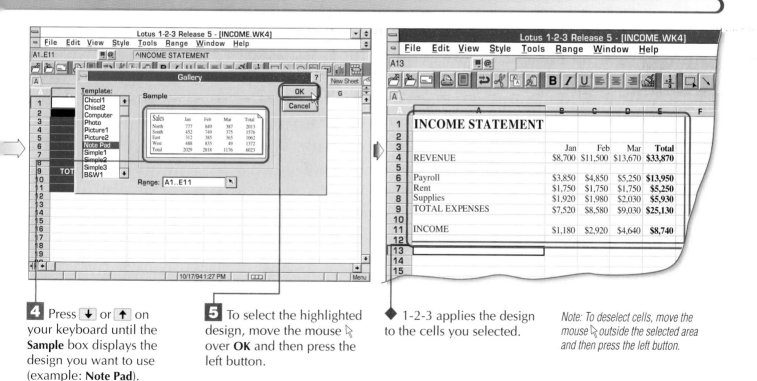

4 Press ⬇ or ⬆ on your keyboard until the **Sample** box displays the design you want to use (example: **Note Pad**).

5 To select the highlighted design, move the mouse ▷ over **OK** and then press the left button.

◆ 1-2-3 applies the design to the cells you selected.

Note: To deselect cells, move the mouse ▷ outside the selected area and then press the left button.

103

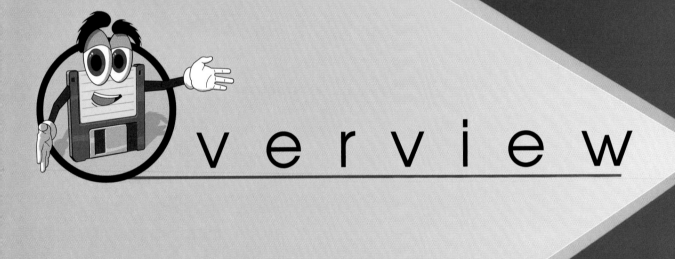

Overview

PRINT YOUR WORKSHEETS

Preview a Worksheet

Print a Worksheet

Add a Page Break

Center Data on a Page

Change Page Orientation

Change Margins

Add Headers and Footers

Change Printed Data Size

Hide or Show Worksheet Elements

Print Titles

◆ In this chapter you will learn how to print your worksheet and select from a variety of print options.

PREVIEW A WORKSHEET

The Print Preview feature lets you see on screen how your worksheet will look when printed.

PREVIEW A WORKSHEET

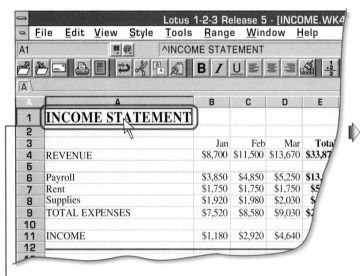

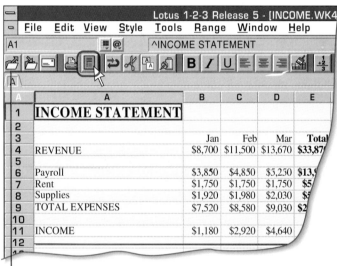

1 To preview your entire worksheet, move the mouse over any cell in the worksheet and then press the left button.

◆ To preview a section of your worksheet, select the cells you want to preview.

Note: To select cells, refer to page 14.

2 Move the mouse over 📄 and then press the left button.

◆ The **Print Preview** dialog box appears.

Getting Started	Save and Open Your Files	Edit Your Worksheets	Using Formulas and Functions	Working with Rows and Columns	Format Your Worksheets	**Print Your Worksheets**

- **Preview a Worksheet**
- Print a Worksheet
- Add a Page Break
- Center Data on a Page
- Change Page Orientation

- Change Margins
- Add Headers and Footers
- Change Printed Data Size
- Hide or Show Worksheet Elements
- Print Titles

Tip

If your worksheet consists of more than one page, you can use these SmartIcons to display other pages in the Print Preview window.

To view the next page, move the mouse ⟶ over and then press the left button.

To view the previous page, move the mouse ⟶ over and then press the left button.

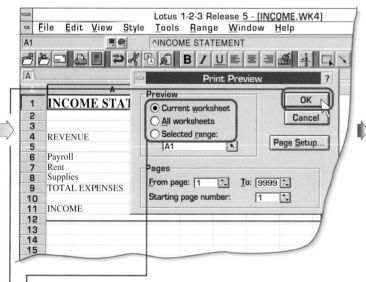

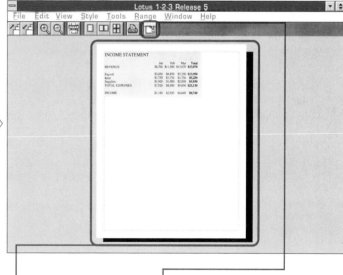

3 Move the mouse ⟶ over the area you want to preview and then press the left button (○ changes to ◉).

4 Move the mouse ⟶ over **OK** and then press the left button.

PREVIEW OPTIONS

Current worksheet
Displays the contents of the current worksheet.

All worksheets
Displays the contents of multiple worksheets.

Selected range:
Displays the cells you selected.

◆ Your worksheet appears in the Print Preview window.

Close Print Preview

1 To close Print Preview and return to your worksheet, move the mouse ⟶ over and then press the left button.

PREVIEW A WORKSHEET

In Print Preview, you can magnify a page to view small details. You can also display multiple pages to view the overall style of a worksheet.

PREVIEW A WORKSHEET

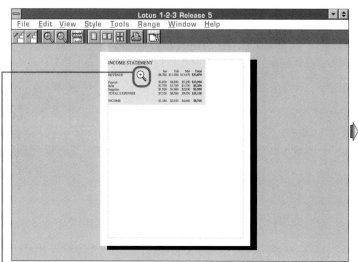

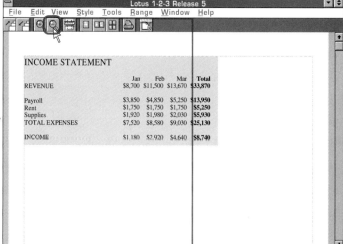

Magnify or Reduce Display

1 To magnify an area of the page, move the mouse ⊕ over the area and then press the left button.

Note: To display your worksheet in the Print Preview window, refer to page 106.

◆ A magnified view of the area appears.

Note: To further magnify the area, repeat step 1.

2 To reduce the display of the area, move the mouse ⊢ over ⊖ and then press the left button.

Getting Started

Save and Open Your Files

Edit Your Worksheets

Using Formulas and Functions

Working with Rows and Columns

Format Your Worksheets

- **Preview a Worksheet**
- Print a Worksheet
- Add a Page Break
- Center Data on a Page
- Change Page Orientation

- Change Margins
- Add Headers and Footers
- Change Printed Data Size
- Hide or Show Worksheet Elements
- Print Titles

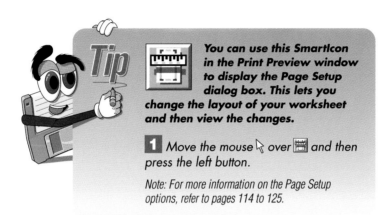

Tip

You can use this SmartIcon in the Print Preview window to display the Page Setup dialog box. This lets you change the layout of your worksheet and then view the changes.

1 *Move the mouse � over ▦ and then press the left button.*

Note: For more information on the Page Setup options, refer to pages 114 to 125.

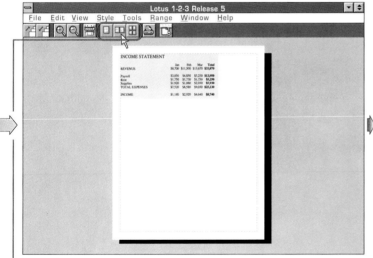

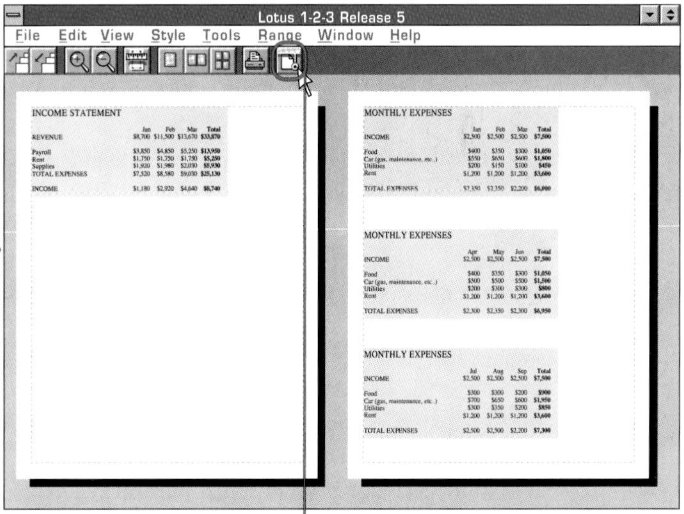

Display Multiple Pages

1 To change the number of pages displayed on your screen, move the mouse � over one of the SmartIcons to the right and then press the left button.

▢ Displays one page.

▦ Displays two pages.

▦ Displays multiple pages.

◆ The number of pages you specified appear.

Note: In this example, the worksheet contains two pages.

Close Print Preview

1 To close Print Preview and return to your worksheet, move the mouse � over ▣ and then press the left button.

PRINT A WORKSHEET

You can print a section of data or your entire worksheet. Before printing, make sure your printer is on and it contains paper.

PRINT A WORKSHEET

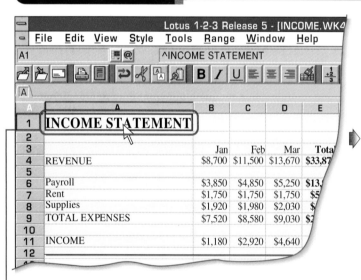

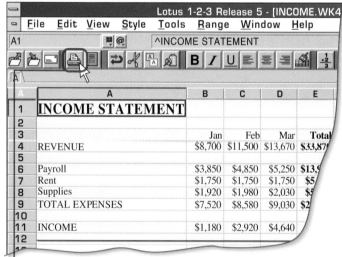

1 To print your entire worksheet, move the mouse over any cell in the worksheet and then press the left button.

◆ To print a section of your worksheet, select the cells you want to print.

Note: To select cells, refer to page 14.

2 Move the mouse over 🖨 and then press the left button.

◆ The **Print** dialog box appears.

| Getting Started | Save and Open Your Files | Edit Your Worksheets | Using Formulas and Functions | Working with Rows and Columns | Format Your Worksheets | **Print Your Worksheets** |

- Preview a Worksheet
- **Print a Worksheet**
- Add a Page Break
- Center Data on a Page
- Change Page Orientation

- Change Margins
- Add Headers and Footers
- Change Printed Data Size
- Hide or Show Worksheet Elements
- Print Titles

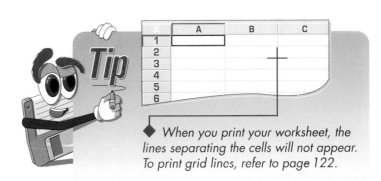

◆ When you print your worksheet, the lines separating the cells will not appear. To print grid lines, refer to page 122.

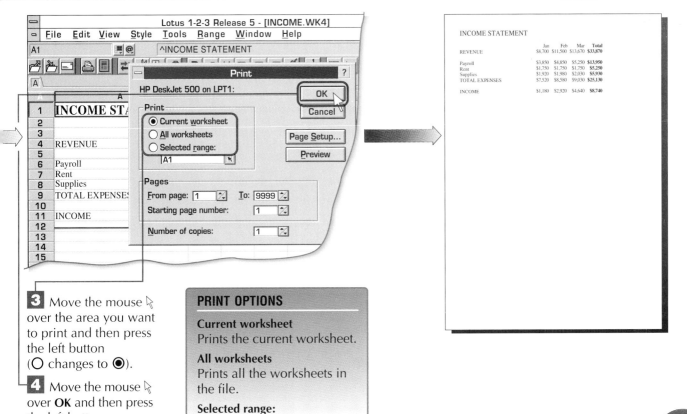

3 Move the mouse ⌗ over the area you want to print and then press the left button (○ changes to ◉).

4 Move the mouse ⌗ over **OK** and then press the left button.

PRINT OPTIONS

Current worksheet
Prints the current worksheet.

All worksheets
Prints all the worksheets in the file.

Selected range:
Prints the cells you selected.

ADD A PAGE BREAK

If you want to start a new page at a specific place in your worksheet, you can add a page break. A page break defines where one page ends and another begins.

A page break you added.

If the data in your worksheet cannot fit on one page, 1-2-3 automatically starts a new page by adding a page break.

A page break 1-2-3 added.

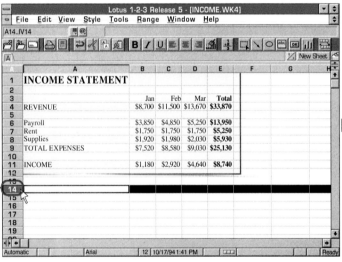

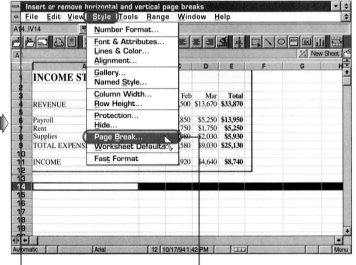

Across a Page

1-2-3 adds a page break above the row you select.

1 To select a row, move the mouse over the row heading (example: **row 14**) and then press the left button.

Down a Page

1-2-3 adds a page break to the left of the column you select.

◆ To select a column, move the mouse over the column heading and then press the left button.

2 Move the mouse over **Style** and then press the left button.

3 Move the mouse over **Page Break** and then press the left button.

◆ The **Page Break** dialog box appears.

INTRODUCTION TO LOTUS 1-2-3

| Getting Started | Save and Open Your Files | Edit Your Worksheets | Using Formulas and Functions | Working with Rows and Columns | Format Your Worksheets | **Print Your Worksheets** |

- Preview a Worksheet
- Print a Worksheet
- **Add a Page Break**
- Center Data on a Page
- Change Page Orientation

- Change Margins
- Add Headers and Footers
- Change Printed Data Size
- Hide or Show Worksheet Elements
- Print Titles

REMOVE A PAGE BREAK

1 To remove a page break, move the mouse ⌖ over any cell directly below or directly to the right of the page break line and then press the left button.

2 Perform steps **2** to **5** below.

*Note: ⊠ changes to ☐ in step **4**.*

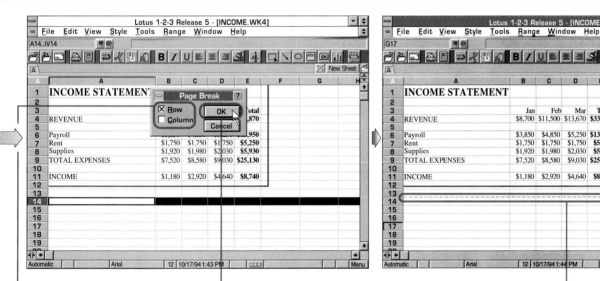
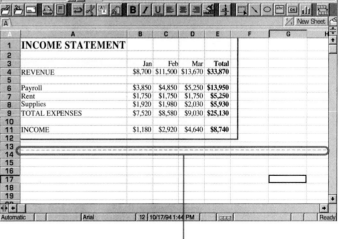

4 To add a page break across the page, move the mouse ⌖ over **Row** and then press the left button (☐ changes to ⊠).

◆ To add a page break down the page, move the mouse ⌖ over **Column** and then press the left button.

5 Move the mouse ⌖ over **OK** and then press the left button.

6 To view the page break, move the mouse ⌖ over any cell in your worksheet and then press the left button.

◆ A dashed line appears on your screen. This line defines where one page ends and another begins.

Note: This line will not appear when you print your worksheet.

CENTER DATA ON A PAGE   CHANGE PAGE ORIENTATION

You can center data across and down a page.

INCOME STATEMENT

CENTER DATA ON A PAGE

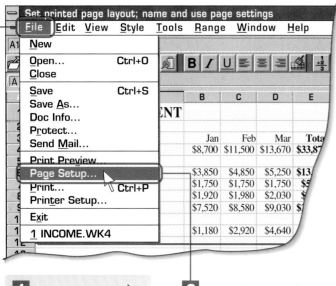

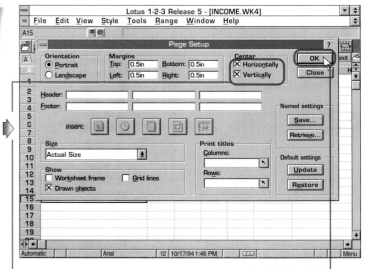

1 Move the mouse over **File** and then press the left button.

2 Move the mouse over **Page Setup** and then press the left button.

◆ The **Page Setup** dialog box appears.

3 To center data across a page, move the mouse over **Horizontally** and then press the left button (□ changes to ⊠).

4 To center data down a page, move the mouse over **Vertically** and then press the left button (□ changes to ⊠).

5 Move the mouse over **OK** and then press the left button.

114

Getting Started	Save and Open Your Files	Edit Your Worksheets	Using Formulas and Functions	Working with Rows and Columns	Format Your Worksheets	**Print Your Worksheets**

- Preview a Worksheet
- Print a Worksheet
- Add a Page Break
- **Center Data on a Page**
- **Change Page Orientation**

- Change Margins
- Add Headers and Footers
- Change Printed Data Size
- Hide or Show Worksheet Elements
- Print Titles

If your worksheet is too wide to fit on one page, you can change to the Landscape orientation to display more data on a page.

Portrait

The worksheet prints across the short side of the paper. This is the initial (or default) setting.

Landscape

The worksheet prints across the long side of the paper.

CHANGE PAGE ORIENTATION

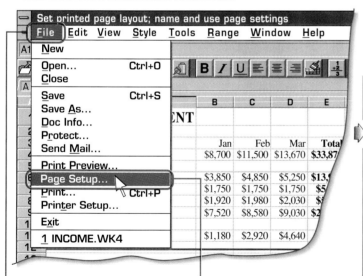

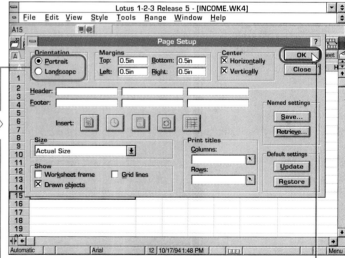

1 Move the mouse ▷ over **File** and then press the left button.

2 Move the mouse ▷ over **Page Setup** and then press the left button.

◆ The **Page Setup** dialog box appears.

3 Move the mouse ▷ over the orientation you want to use and then press the left button (○ changes to ◉).

4 Move the mouse ▷ over **OK** and then press the left button.

CHANGE MARGINS

A margin is the amount of space between data and the edges of your paper. You can use the Page Setup feature to change the margins.

When you begin a worksheet, the top, bottom, left and right margins are all set at 0.5 inches.

CHANGE MARGINS

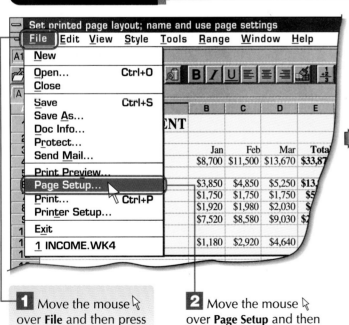

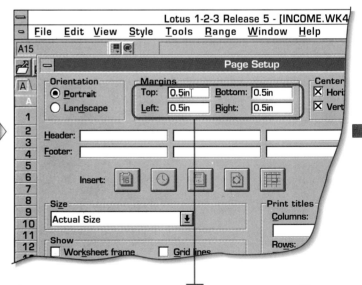

1 Move the mouse ⌖ over **File** and then press the left button.

2 Move the mouse ⌖ over **Page Setup** and then press the left button.

◆ The **Page Setup** dialog box appears.

3 Move the mouse ⌶ over the box beside the margin you want to change (example: **Top**) and then press the left button.

116

Getting Started	Save and Open Your Files	Edit Your Worksheets	Using Formulas and Functions	Working with Rows and Columns	Format Your Worksheets	**Print Your Worksheets**

- Preview a Worksheet
- Print a Worksheet
- Add a Page Break
- Center Data on a Page
- Change Page Orientation

- **Change Margins**
- Add Headers and Footers
- Change Printed Data Size
- Hide or Show Worksheet Elements
- Print Titles

To view the new margins, you can display your worksheet in the Print Preview window.

Note: For more information on the Print Preview feature, refer to pages 106 to 109.

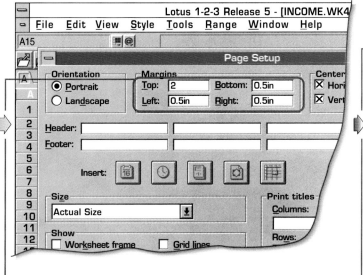

4 Press **◆Backspace** or **Delete** to remove the existing margin.

5 Type a new margin in inches (example: **2**).

◆ Repeat steps **3** to **5** for each margin you want to change.

6 Move the mouse ⌖ over **OK** and then press the left button.

ADD HEADERS AND FOOTERS

> Headers and footers print information at the top and bottom of each page. This information may include the title of your worksheet, the date or your company name.

◆ Header

◆ Footer

ADD HEADERS AND FOOTERS

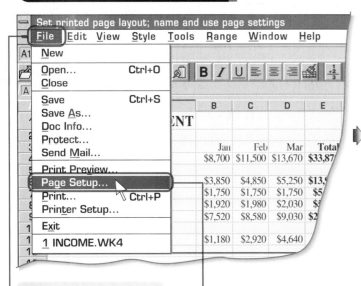

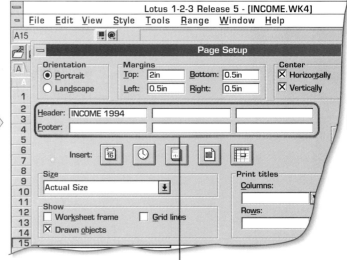

1 Move the mouse ▷ over **File** and then press the left button.

2 Move the mouse ▷ over **Page Setup** and then press the left button.

◆ The **Page Setup** dialog box appears.

3 Move the mouse I over the box for the area of the page where you want to display a header or footer and then press the left button.

*Note: For more information, refer to the **Tip** on page 119.*

4 Type the header or footer text (example: **INCOME 1994**).

Getting Started	Save and Open Your Files	Edit Your Worksheets	Using Formulas and Functions	Working with Rows and Columns	Format Your Worksheets	**Print Your Worksheets**

Working with Rows and Columns / Using Formulas and Functions:
- Preview a Worksheet
- Print a Worksheet
- Add a Page Break
- Center Data on a Page
- Change Page Orientation

Format Your Worksheets / Print Your Worksheets:
- Change Margins
- **Add Headers and Footers**
- Change Printed Data Size
- Hide or Show Worksheet Elements
- Print Titles

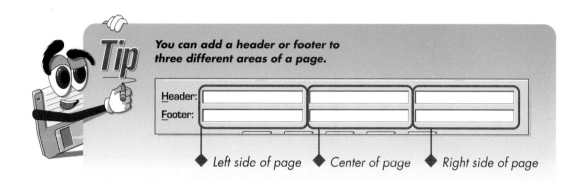

Tip

You can add a header or footer to three different areas of a page.

Header:
Footer:

◆ *Left side of page* ◆ *Center of page* ◆ *Right side of page*

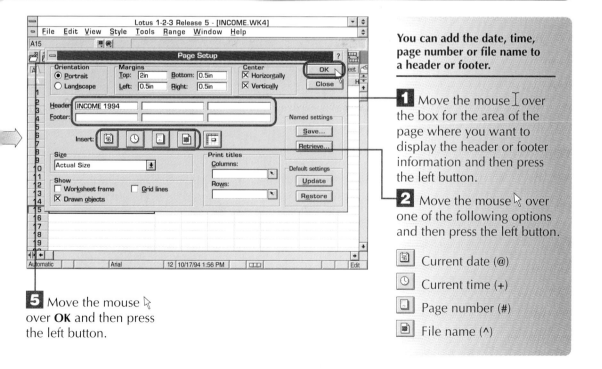

You can add the date, time, page number or file name to a header or footer.

1 Move the mouse I over the box for the area of the page where you want to display the header or footer information and then press the left button.

2 Move the mouse ⇗ over one of the following options and then press the left button.

Current date (@)

Current time (+)

Page number (#)

File name (^)

5 Move the mouse ⇗ over **OK** and then press the left button.

CHANGE PRINTED DATA SIZE

You can increase or decrease the size of data on a printed page. This is useful when you want to fit your data on a specific number of pages.

CHANGE PRINTED DATA SIZE

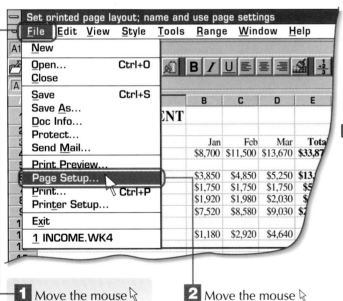

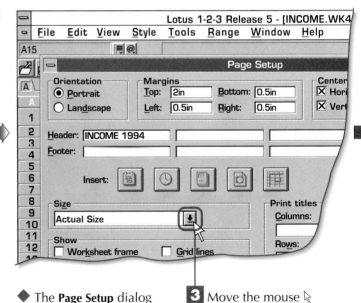

1 Move the mouse ⌖ over **File** and then press the left button.

2 Move the mouse ⌖ over **Page Setup** and then press the left button.

◆ The **Page Setup** dialog box appears.

3 Move the mouse ⌖ over ⬇ below **Size** and then press the left button.

120

INTRODUCTION TO LOTUS 1-2-3

| Getting Started | Save and Open Your Files | Edit Your Worksheets | Using Formulas and Functions | Working with Rows and Columns | Format Your Worksheets | **Print Your Worksheets** |

- Preview a Worksheet
- Print a Worksheet
- Add a Page Break
- Center Data on a Page
- Change Page Orientation

- Change Margins
- Add Headers and Footers
- **Change Printed Data Size**
- Hide or Show Worksheet Elements
- Print Titles

DATA SIZE OPTIONS

Actual Size

Prints the worksheet without increasing or decreasing the data size.

Fit all to page

Decreases the size of data to print the entire worksheet on one page.

Fit columns to page

Decreases the size of data to print all the columns in the worksheet on one page.

Fit rows to page

Decreases the size of data to print all the rows in the worksheet on one page.

Manually scale

Increases or decreases the size of data according to the percentage you specify.

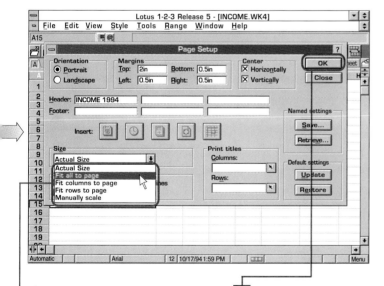

◆ A list of size options appears.

4 Move the mouse ⬚ over the size option you want to use (example: **Fit all to page**) and then press the left button.

*Note: If you selected **Manually scale** in step **4**, refer to "Manually Scale Your Data" to the right.*

5 Move the mouse ⬚ over **OK** and then press the left button.

MANUALLY SCALE YOUR DATA

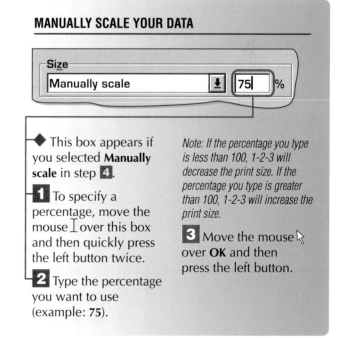

◆ This box appears if you selected **Manually scale** in step **4**.

1 To specify a percentage, move the mouse I over this box and then quickly press the left button twice.

2 Type the percentage you want to use (example: **75**).

Note: If the percentage you type is less than 100, 1-2-3 will decrease the print size. If the percentage you type is greater than 100, 1-2-3 will increase the print size.

3 Move the mouse ⬚ over **OK** and then press the left button.

HIDE OR SHOW WORKSHEET ELEMENTS

Worksheet frame

Grid lines

When you print your worksheet, you can have 1-2-3 display the worksheet frame and grid lines. This can make your printed data easier to review.

HIDE OR SHOW WORKSHEET ELEMENTS

You can hide or display the following options on your printed worksheet.

Worksheet frame
Prints the row and column headings.

Drawn objects
Prints any charts, shapes or lines in your worksheet.

Grid lines
Prints lines that separate the cells in your worksheet.

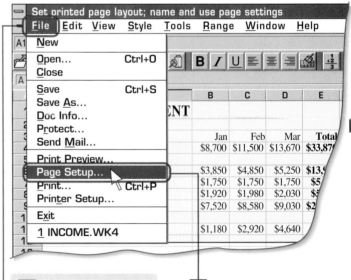

1 Move the mouse ᐅ over **File** and then press the left button.

2 Move the mouse ᐅ over **Page Setup** and then press the left button.

Getting Started	Save and Open Your Files	Edit Your Worksheets	Using Formulas and Functions	Working with Rows and Columns	Format Your Worksheets	**Print Your Worksheets**

- Preview a Worksheet
- Print a Worksheet
- Add a Page Break
- Center Data on a Page
- Change Page Orientation

- Change Margins
- Add Headers and Footers
- Change Printed Data Size
- **Hide or Show Worksheet Elements**
- Print Titles

You can add shapes and lines to your worksheet to emphasize data.

Note: For more information, refer to page 188.

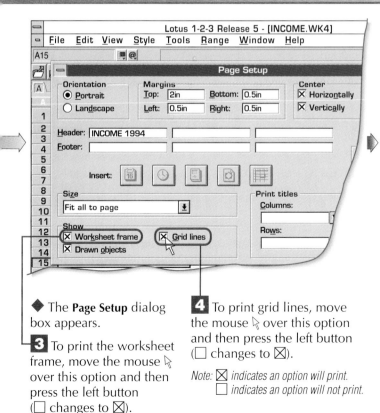

◆ The **Page Setup** dialog box appears.

3 To print the worksheet frame, move the mouse ↖ over this option and then press the left button (☐ changes to ☒).

4 To print grid lines, move the mouse ↖ over this option and then press the left button (☐ changes to ☒).

Note: ☒ indicates an option will print.
☐ indicates an option will not print.

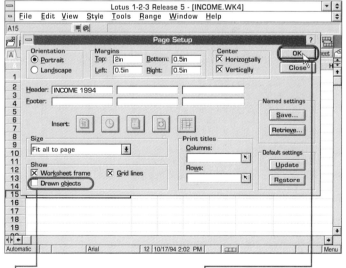

5 Drawn objects will appear when you print your worksheet. If you do not want to print drawn objects, move the mouse ↖ over this option and then press the left button. (☒ changes to ☐).

6 Move the mouse ↖ over **OK** and then press the left button.

PRINT TITLES

You can use the headings from your worksheet as titles on each printed page. This helps you review your printed data in worksheets that contain multiple pages.

PRINT TITLES DOWN EACH PAGE

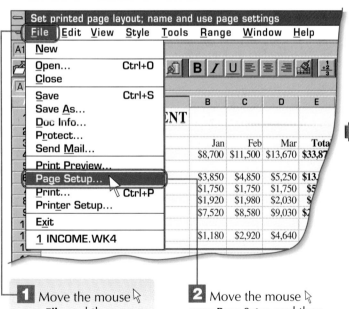

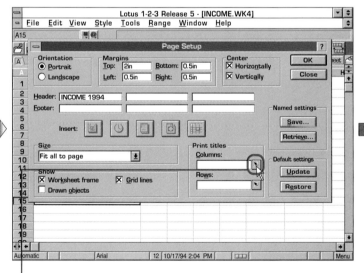

1 Move the mouse over **File** and then press the left button.

2 Move the mouse over **Page Setup** and then press the left button.

◆ The **Page Setup** dialog box appears.

3 To print titles down the left side of each printed page, move the mouse over ▣ below **Columns:** and then press the left button.

Note: To print titles across the top of each printed page, refer to "Print Titles Across Each Page" on page 125.

Getting
Started

Save and
Open Your
Files

Edit Your
Worksheets

Using
Formulas
and Functions

Working with
Rows and
Columns

Format Your
Worksheets

**Print Your
Worksheets**

- Preview a Worksheet
- Print a Worksheet
- Add a Page Break
- Center Data on a Page
- Change Page Orientation

- Change Margins
- Add Headers and Footers
- Change Printed Data Size
- Hide or Show Worksheet Elements
- **Print Titles**

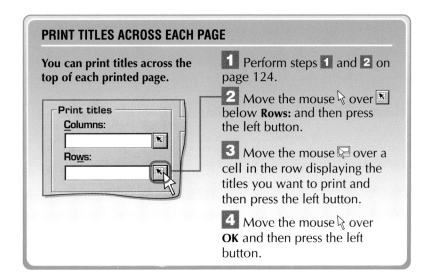

PRINT TITLES ACROSS EACH PAGE

**You can print titles across the
top of each printed page.**

1 Perform steps **1** and **2** on
page 124.

2 Move the mouse over
below **Rows:** and then press
the left button.

3 Move the mouse over a
cell in the row displaying the
titles you want to print and
then press the left button.

4 Move the mouse over
OK and then press the left
button.

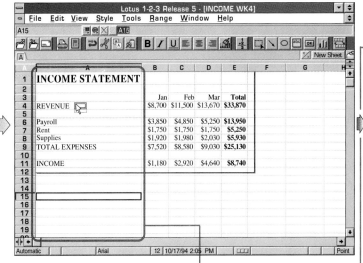

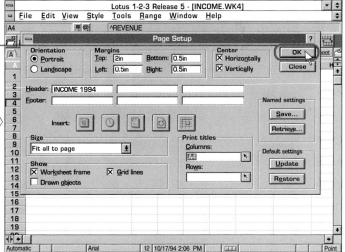

◆ The dialog box
temporarily disappears
so you can view the
cells in your worksheet.

4 Move the mouse
over a cell in the column
displaying the titles you
want to print (example:
column A) and then press
the left button.

◆ The dialog box reappears.

5 Move the mouse over
OK and then press the left
button.

*Note: When you print your worksheet,
the titles will appear twice on the first
page. To avoid this, delete the titles on
the first page before printing.*

verview

CHANGE YOUR SCREEN DISPLAY

Zoom In or Out

Display Different SmartIcons

Freeze Titles

Split the Screen

◆ In this chapter you will learn how to change the way your worksheet appears on screen.

ZOOM IN OR OUT

You can magnify a worksheet to read small data or reduce a worksheet to view more of your data.

ZOOM IN

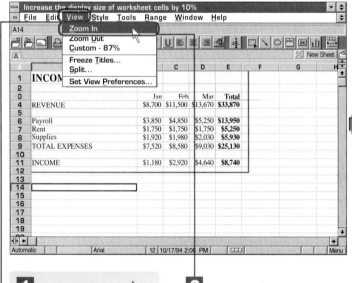

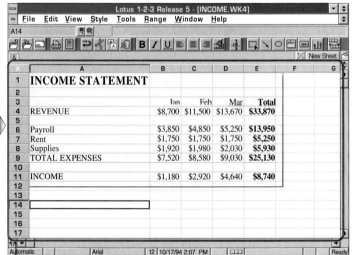

1 Move the mouse over **View** and then press the left button.

2 To magnify your worksheet, move the mouse over **Zoom In** and then press the left button.

◆ Your worksheet is magnified by 10%.

◆ To further magnify your worksheet, repeat steps **1** and **2**.

Note: When you zoom your worksheet in or out, the change will not affect the way your worksheet appears on a printed page.

Change Your Screen Display	Using Multiple Worksheets	Using Multiple Files	Charting Data	Drawing Objects	Working With Databases

- **Zoom In or Out**
- Display Different SmartIcons
- Freeze Titles
- Split the Screen

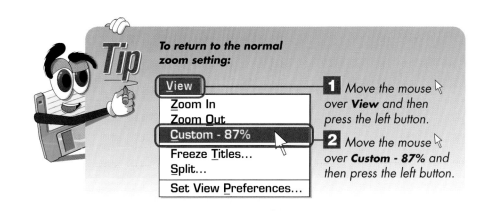

To return to the normal zoom setting:

View
Zoom In
Zoom Out
Custom - 87%
Freeze Titles...
Split...
Set View Preferences...

1 Move the mouse over **View** and then press the left button.

2 Move the mouse over **Custom - 87%** and then press the left button.

ZOOM OUT

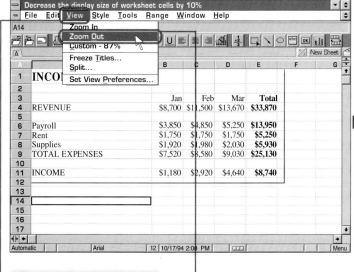

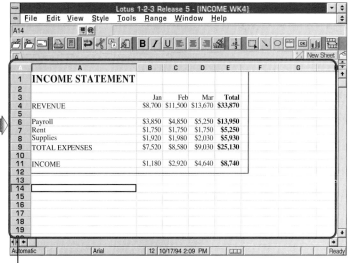

1 Move the mouse over **View** and then press the left button.

2 To reduce your worksheet, move the mouse over **Zoom Out** and then press the left button.

◆ Your worksheet is reduced by 10%.

◆ To further reduce your worksheet, repeat steps **1** and **2**.

DISPLAY DIFFERENT SMARTICONS

> SmartIcons let you quickly select commonly used commands. 1-2-3 offers eight sets of SmartIcons, each related to a specific task.

DISPLAY DIFFERENT SMARTICONS (METHOD 1)

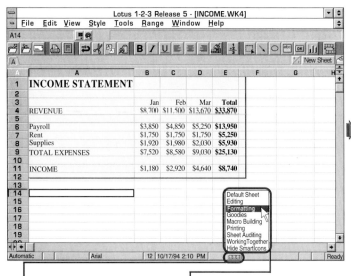

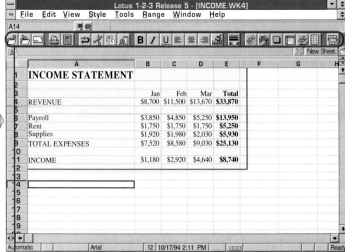

1 To display a list of SmartIcon sets, move the mouse ▷ over ▭ and then press the left button.

2 Move the mouse ▷ over the SmartIcon set you want to display (example: **Formatting**) and then press the left button.

◆ The SmartIcon set you selected appears.

*Note: To return to the original SmartIcon set, repeat steps **1** and **2**, selecting **Default Sheet** in step **2**.*

Change Your Screen Display	Using Multiple Worksheets	Using Multiple Files	Charting Data	Drawing Objects	Working With Databases

- Zoom In or Out
- **Display Different SmartIcons**
- Freeze Titles
- Split the Screen

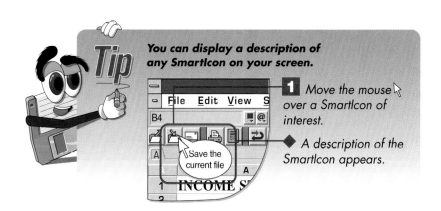

You can display a description of any SmartIcon on your screen.

1 Move the mouse over a SmartIcon of interest.

◆ A description of the SmartIcon appears.

DISPLAY DIFFERENT SMARTICONS (METHOD 2)

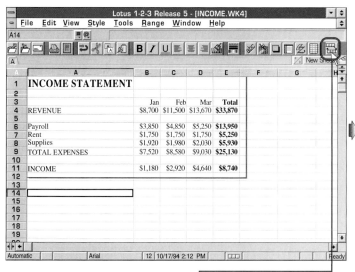

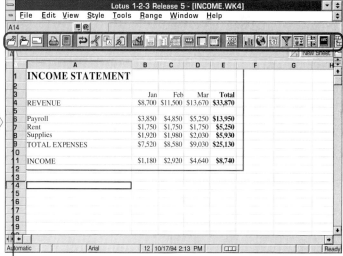

You can quickly cycle through all of the SmartIcon sets.

1 To display the next set of SmartIcons, move the mouse over 🔲 and then press the left button.

◆ The next set of SmartIcons appears.

2 Repeat step **1** until the set you want to use appears.

Note: You will cycle through the SmartIcon sets and eventually return to the original set.

131

FREEZE TITLES

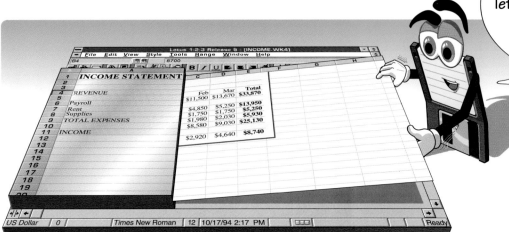

You can freeze titles in your worksheet so they will not move. This lets you keep your titles on screen as you move through data in a large worksheet.

FREEZE TITLES

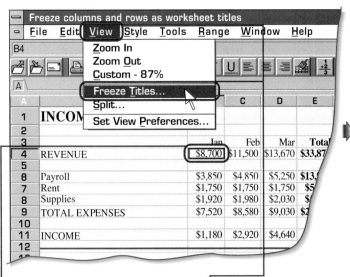

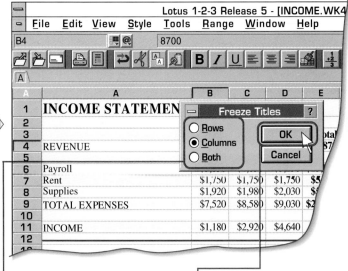

1 To freeze columns, move the mouse ⇩ over a cell directly to the right of the column(s) you want to freeze and then press the left button.

Note: To freeze rows, move the mouse ⇩ over a cell directly below the row(s) you want to freeze and then press the left button.

2 Move the mouse ⇩ over **View** and then press the left button.

3 Move the mouse ⇩ over **Freeze Titles** and then press the left button.

◆ The **Freeze Titles** dialog box appears.

4 Move the mouse ⇩ over the area you want to freeze (example: **Columns**) and then press the left button. ○ changes to ◉.

5 Move the mouse ⇩ over **OK** and then press the left button.

- Zoom In or Out
- Display Different SmartIcons
- **Freeze Titles**
- Split the Screen

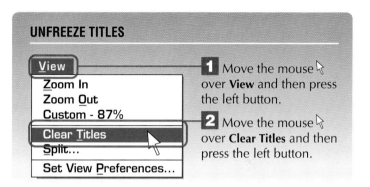

UNFREEZE TITLES

1 Move the mouse over **View** and then press the left button.

2 Move the mouse over **Clear Titles** and then press the left button.

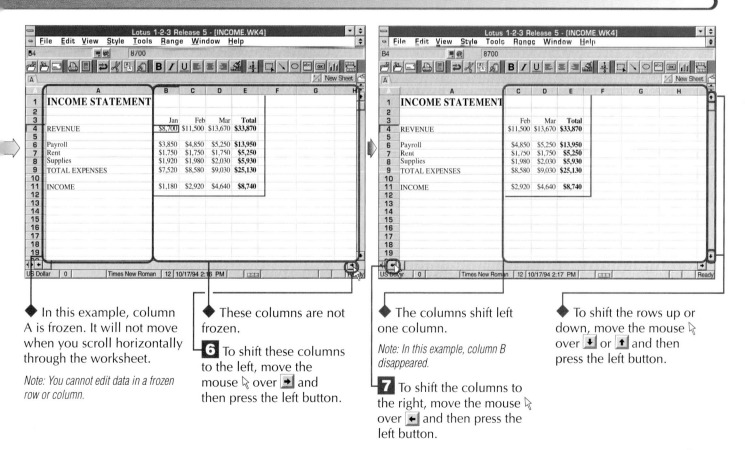

◆ In this example, column A is frozen. It will not move when you scroll horizontally through the worksheet.

Note: You cannot edit data in a frozen row or column.

◆ These columns are not frozen.

6 To shift these columns to the left, move the mouse over ➡ and then press the left button.

◆ The columns shift left one column.

Note: In this example, column B disappeared.

7 To shift the columns to the right, move the mouse over ⬅ and then press the left button.

◆ To shift the rows up or down, move the mouse over ⬇ or ⬆ and then press the left button.

SPLIT THE SCREEN

You can split your screen in two separate sections. This lets you view different areas of a large worksheet at the same time.

SPLIT THE SCREEN VERTICALLY

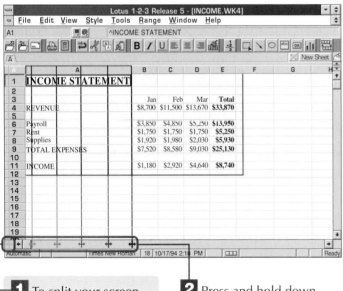

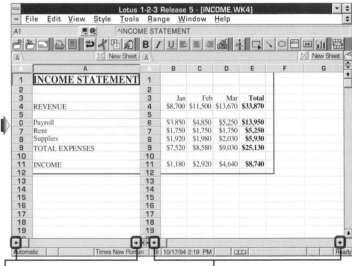

1 To split your screen vertically in two sections, move the mouse ⌖ over ◀▶ and ⌖ changes to ✛.

2 Press and hold down the left button as you move the mouse ✛ where you want to split the screen.

3 Release the button and the screen splits vertically in two.

◆ To move through the columns in the left window, move the mouse ⌖ over ➡ or ◀ and then press the left button.

◆ To move through the columns in the right window, move the mouse ⌖ over ➡ or ◀ and then press the left button.

Note: To clear the split, refer to the top of page 135.

Change Your Screen Display	Using Multiple Worksheets	Using Multiple Files	Charting Data	Drawing Objects	Working With Databases

- Zoom In or Out
- Display Different SmartIcons
- Freeze Titles
- **Split the Screen**

CLEAR THE SPLIT

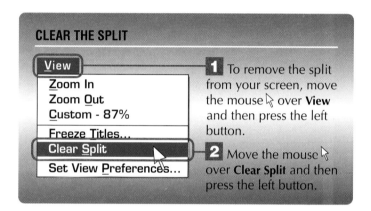

1 To remove the split from your screen, move the mouse ⬡ over **View** and then press the left button.

2 Move the mouse ⬡ over **Clear Split** and then press the left button.

SPLIT THE SCREEN HORIZONTALLY

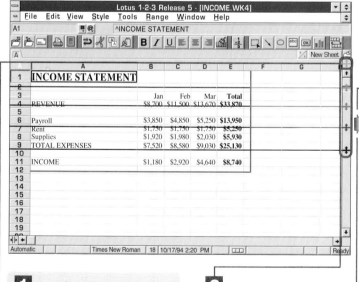

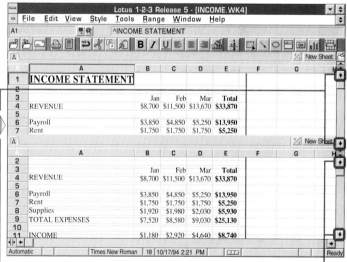

1 To split your screen horizontally in two sections, move the mouse ⬡ over ⬍ and ⬡ changes to ✛.

2 Press and hold down the left button as you move the mouse ✛ where you want to split the screen.

3 Release the button and the screen splits horizontally in two.

◆ To move through the rows in the top window, move the mouse ⬡ over ⬇ or ⬆ and then press the left button.

◆ To move through the rows in the bottom window, move the mouse ⬡ over ⬇ or ⬆ and then press the left button.

Overview

USING MULTIPLE WORKSHEETS

Insert a Worksheet

Switch Between Worksheets

Name a Worksheet

View Multiple Worksheets

Copy or Move Data Between Worksheets

Delete a Worksheet

Enter a Formula Across Worksheets

Link Data Across Worksheets

◆ In this chapter you will learn how to work with more than one worksheet in a file.

INSERT A WORKSHEET

A file is like a three-ring binder that contains many sheets. You can add worksheets at any time to store new information.

INSERT A WORKSHEET

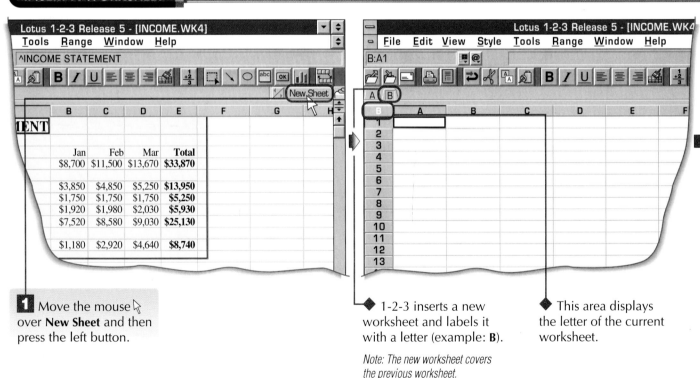

1 Move the mouse ⊳ over **New Sheet** and then press the left button.

◆ 1-2-3 inserts a new worksheet and labels it with a letter (example: **B**).

Note: The new worksheet covers the previous worksheet.

◆ This area displays the letter of the current worksheet.

| Change Your Screen Display | Using Multiple Worksheets | Using Multiple Files | Charting Data | Drawing Objects | Working With Databases |

- **Insert a Worksheet**
- Switch Between Worksheets
- Name a Worksheet
- View Multiple Worksheets
- Copy or Move Data Between Worksheets
- Delete a Worksheet
- Enter a Formula Across Worksheets
- Link Data Across Worksheets

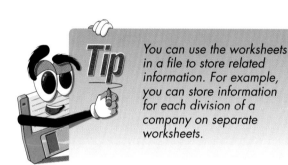

Tip

You can use the worksheets in a file to store related information. For example, you can store information for each division of a company on separate worksheets.

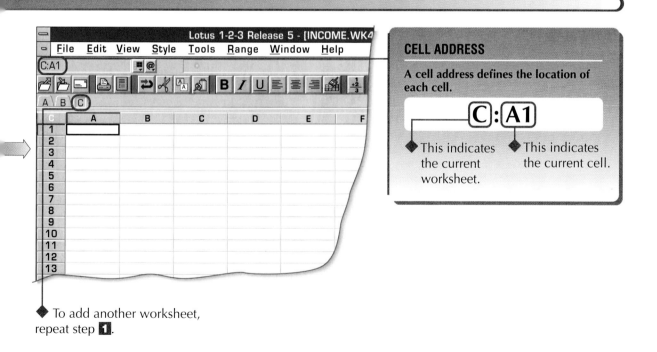

CELL ADDRESS

A cell address defines the location of each cell.

$$C:A1$$

◆ This indicates the current worksheet.

◆ This indicates the current cell.

◆ To add another worksheet, repeat step **1**.

You can easily switch between all of the worksheets in a file. This lets you view the contents of each worksheet.

SWITCH BETWEEN WORKSHEETS

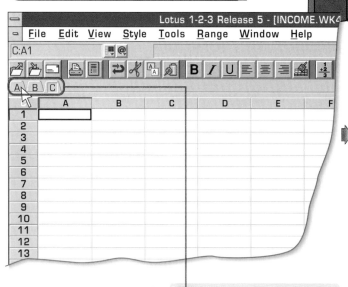

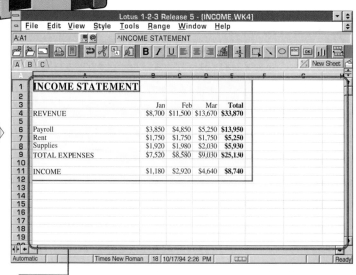

◆ The contents of the current worksheet are displayed on your screen. The contents of the other worksheets are hidden behind this worksheet.

1 To display the contents of another worksheet, move the mouse ⏳ over the worksheet tab (example: **A**) and then press the left button.

◆ The contents of the worksheet appear.

Change Your Screen Display	Using Multiple Worksheets	Using Multiple Files	Charting Data	Drawing Objects	Working With Databases

- Insert a Worksheet
- **Switch Between Worksheets**
- **Name a Worksheet**
- View Multiple Worksheets
- Copy or Move Data Between Worksheets
- Delete a Worksheet
- Enter a Formula Across Worksheets
- Link Data Across Worksheets

> You can give each worksheet in a file a descriptive name. This helps you remember where you stored your data.

NAME A WORKSHEET

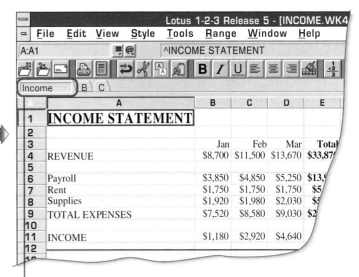

1 To change the name of a worksheet, move the mouse over the worksheet tab and then quickly press the left button twice.

2 Type a name for the worksheet (example: **Income**).

3 Press `Enter` on your keyboard.

VIEW MULTIPLE WORKSHEETS

If you have several worksheets in a file, some of them may be hidden from view. You can use the Split command to view the contents of three worksheets at the same time.

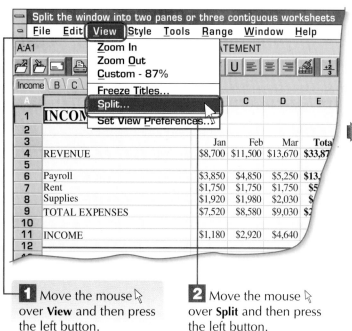

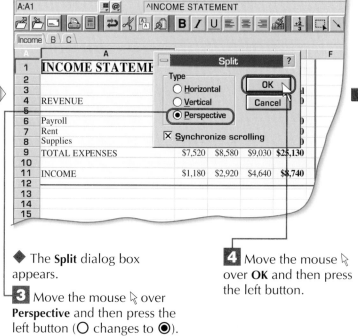

1 Move the mouse ↖ over **View** and then press the left button.

2 Move the mouse ↖ over **Split** and then press the left button.

◆ The **Split** dialog box appears.

3 Move the mouse ↖ over **Perspective** and then press the left button (○ changes to ◉).

4 Move the mouse ↖ over **OK** and then press the left button.

Change
Your Screen
Display

**Using
Multiple
Worksheets**

Using
Multiple Files

Charting
Data

Drawing
Objects

Working With
Databases

• Insert a Worksheet
• Switch Between Worksheets
• Name a Worksheet
• **View Multiple Worksheets**

• Copy or Move Data Between Worksheets
• Delete a Worksheet
• Enter a Formula Across Worksheets
• Link Data Across Worksheets

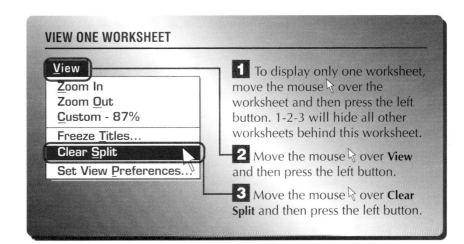

VIEW ONE WORKSHEET

View
Zoom In
Zoom Out
Custom - 87%
Freeze Titles...
Clear Split
Set View Preferences...

1 To display only one worksheet, move the mouse over the worksheet and then press the left button. 1-2-3 will hide all other worksheets behind this worksheet.

2 Move the mouse over **View** and then press the left button.

3 Move the mouse over **Clear Split** and then press the left button.

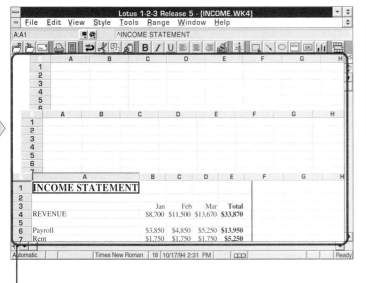

♦ You can now view the contents of your worksheets.

The Split feature can only display three worksheets on your screen at once. If your file contains more than three worksheets, you can use your keyboard to display the other worksheets.

♦ Press **Ctrl** + **PageUp** to display the next worksheet in the file.

♦ Press **Ctrl** + **PageDown** to display the previous worksheet in the file.

COPY OR MOVE DATA BETWEEN WORKSHEETS

Copying or moving data between worksheets saves you time when you are working in one worksheet and want to use data from another.

COPY OR MOVE DATA BETWEEN WORKSHEETS

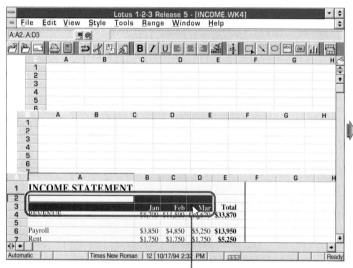

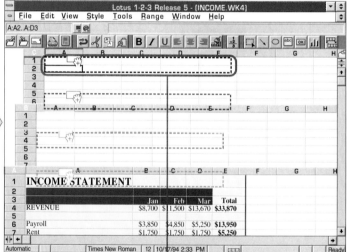

1 Display the worksheets you want to copy or move data between.

Note: To display multiple worksheets, refer to page 142.

2 Select the cells you want to copy or move to another worksheet.

Note: To select cells, refer to page 14.

3 Move the mouse ➢ over a border of the cells you selected and ➢ changes to ⌐ᵐ⌐.

4 To copy the data, press and hold down `Ctrl` and press and hold down the left button as you drag the mouse ⌐⁺⌐ where you want to place the data.

◆ To move the data, press and hold down the left button as you drag the mouse ⌐⁺⌐ where you want to place the data.

| Change
Your Screen
Display | Using
Multiple
Worksheets | Using
Multiple Files | Charting
Data | Drawing
Objects | Working With
Databases |

- Insert a Worksheet
- Switch Between Worksheets
- Name a Worksheet
- View Multiple Worksheets
- **Copy or Move Data Between Worksheets**
- Delete a Worksheet
- Enter a Formula Across Worksheets
- Link Data Across Worksheets

The Copy and Move features both place data in a new location, but they have one distinct difference.

COPY DATA

When you copy data, the original data remains in its place.

MOVE DATA

When you move data, the original data disappears.

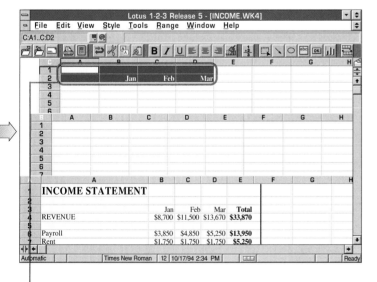

5 Release the left button (and **Ctrl**) and the data appears in the new location.

   You can also use these SmartIcons to copy or move data.

1 Perform steps **1** and **2** on page 144.

2 To copy data, position the mouse ⬚ over ▣ and then press the left button.

◆ To move data, position the mouse ⬚ over ▣ and then press the left button.

3 Select the cell where you want to place the data. This cell will become the top left cell of the new location.

4 Move the mouse ⬚ over ▣ and then press the left button. The data appears in the new location.

DELETE A WORKSHEET

You can permanently remove a worksheet that you no longer need.

DELETE A WORKSHEET

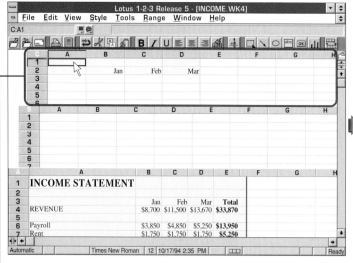

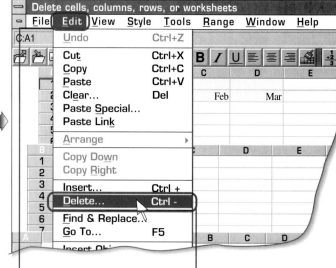

1 Move the mouse ⬚ over any cell in the worksheet you want to delete and then press the left button.

2 Move the mouse ⬚ over **Edit** and then press the left button.

3 Move the mouse ⬚ over **Delete** and then press the left button.

◆ The **Delete** dialog box appears.

Change Your Screen Display	Using Multiple Worksheets	Using Multiple Files	Charting Data	Drawing Objects	Working With Databases

• Insert a Worksheet
• Switch Between Worksheets
• Name a Worksheet
• View Multiple Worksheets

• Copy or Move Data Between Worksheets
• **Delete a Worksheet**
• Enter a Formula Across Worksheets
• Link Data Across Worksheets

IMPORTANT!

Do not delete a worksheet you may need in the future. Once you delete a worksheet, 1-2-3 erases the data from your computer's memory.

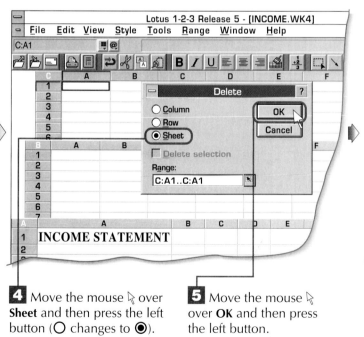

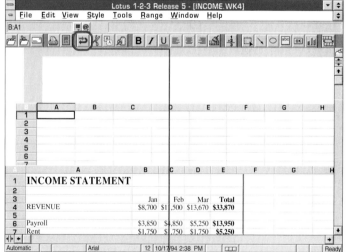

4 Move the mouse ⌖ over **Sheet** and then press the left button (○ changes to ◉).

5 Move the mouse ⌖ over **OK** and then press the left button.

◆ The worksheet disappears from your screen.

Undo the Deletion

◆ To immediately restore the deleted worksheet, move the mouse ⌖ over ⇄ and then press the left button.

ENTER A FORMULA ACROSS WORKSHEETS

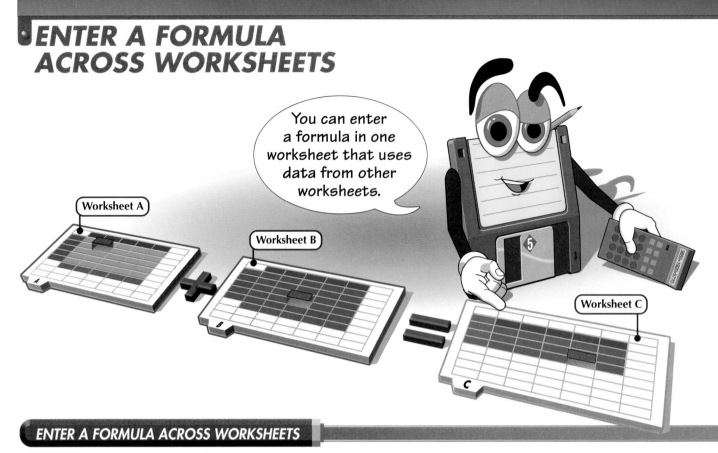

You can enter a formula in one worksheet that uses data from other worksheets.

Worksheet A

Worksheet B

Worksheet C

ENTER A FORMULA ACROSS WORKSHEETS

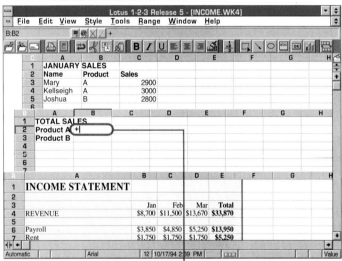

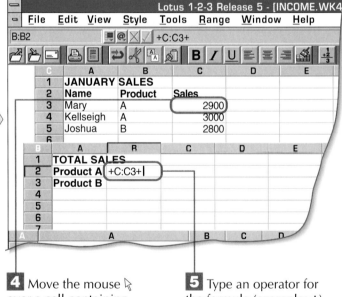

1 Display the worksheets containing the data you want to include in the formula.

Note: To insert a worksheet, refer to page 138. To display multiple worksheets, refer to page 142.

2 Move the mouse over the cell where you want to display the result of the formula and then press the left button.

3 To begin the formula, type a plus sign (+).

4 Move the mouse over a cell containing data you want to use in the formula and then press the left button.

5 Type an operator for the formula (example: +).

| Change Your Screen Display | Using Multiple Worksheets | Using Multiple Files | Charting Data | Drawing Objects | Working With Databases |

- Insert a Worksheet
- Switch Between Worksheets
- Name a Worksheet
- View Multiple Worksheets
- Copy or Move Data Between Worksheets
- Delete a Worksheet
- **Enter a Formula Across Worksheets**
- Link Data Across Worksheets

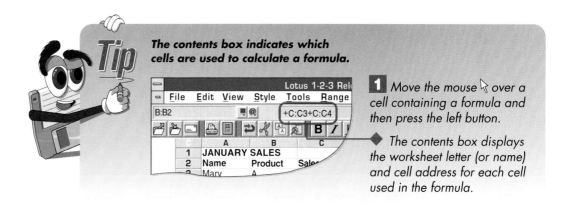

The contents box indicates which cells are used to calculate a formula.

1 Move the mouse over a cell containing a formula and then press the left button.

◆ The contents box displays the worksheet letter (or name) and cell address for each cell used in the formula.

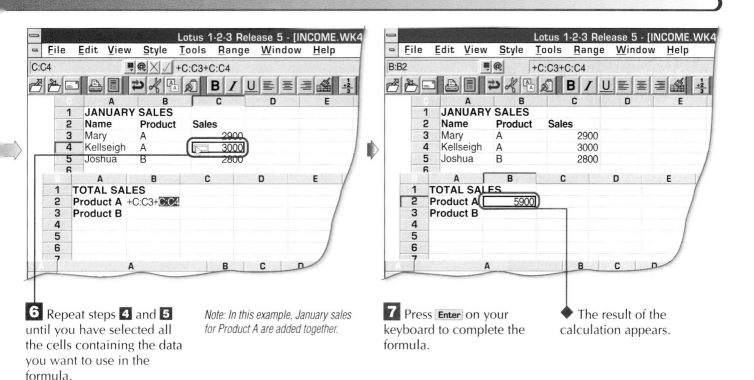

6 Repeat steps **4** and **5** until you have selected all the cells containing the data you want to use in the formula.

Note: In this example, January sales for Product A are added together.

7 Press [Enter] on your keyboard to complete the formula.

◆ The result of the calculation appears.

LINK DATA ACROSS WORKSHEETS

If you want a worksheet to always display the same data as another, you can link the data.

Original Worksheet

Data Linked to Original Worksheet

If you change the data in the original worksheet, the data in all linked worksheets will also change.

LINK DATA ACROSS WORKSHEETS

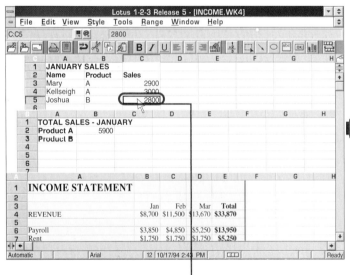

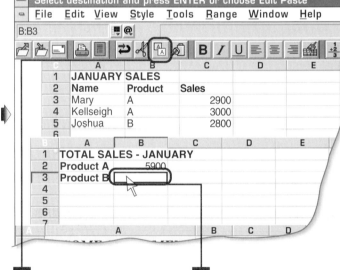

1 Display the worksheets you want to contain the same data.

Note: To display multiple worksheets, refer to page 142.

2 Move the mouse ⬚ over the cell that contains the data you want to link to another worksheet and then press the left button.

3 To copy the data, move the mouse ⬚ over 🔲 and then press the left button.

4 Move the mouse ⬚ over the cell where you want to place the data and then press the left button.

| Change Your Screen Display | Using Multiple Worksheets | Using Multiple Files | Charting Data | Drawing Objects | Working With Databases |

- Insert a Worksheet
- Switch Between Worksheets
- Name a Worksheet
- View Multiple Worksheets
- Copy or Move Data Between Worksheets
- Delete a Worksheet
- Enter a Formula Across Worksheets
- **Link Data Across Worksheets**

The Copy and Link features both place a copy of data in a new location, but they have one distinct difference.

COPY DATA

When you copy data, the data is not connected. If you change the data in the original worksheet, the data in the other worksheet will not change.

LINK DATA

When you link data, the data is connected. If you change the data in the original worksheet, the data in the linked worksheet will also change.

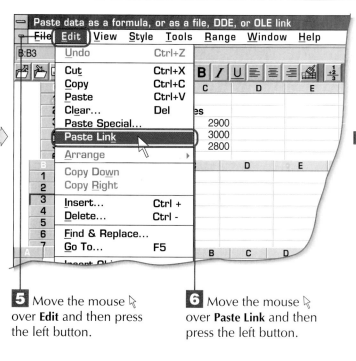

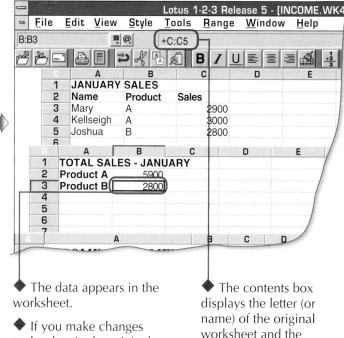

5 Move the mouse � over **Edit** and then press the left button.

6 Move the mouse � over **Paste Link** and then press the left button.

◆ The data appears in the worksheet.

◆ If you make changes to the data in the original worksheet, the linked data will automatically display the change.

◆ The contents box displays the letter (or name) of the original worksheet and the linked cell.

USING MULTIPLE FILES

Create a New File

Cascade Files

Tile Files

Maximize a File

Switch Between Files

Close a File

Using a SmartMaster

◆ In this chapter you will learn how to create a new file and work with more than one file at a time.

CREATE A NEW FILE

You can create a new file to store data on a different topic.

CREATE A NEW FILE

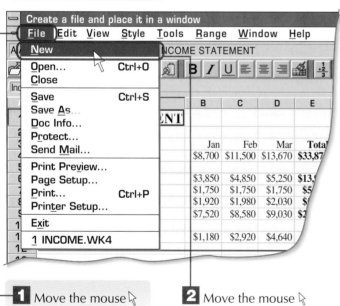

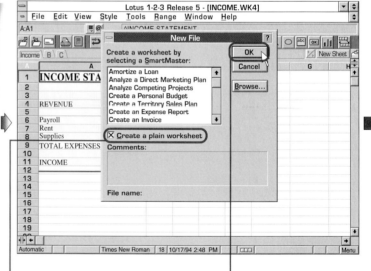

1 Move the mouse ℏ over **File** and then press the left button.

2 Move the mouse ℏ over **New** and then press the left button.

◆ The **New File** dialog box appears.

3 To create a new file, move the mouse ℏ over this option and then press the left button (☐ changes to ☒).

4 Move the mouse ℏ over **OK** and then press the left button.

Change Your Screen Display	Using Multiple Worksheets	**Using Multiple Files**	Charting Data	Drawing Objects	Working With Databases

- **Create a New File**
- Cascade Files
- Tile Files
- Maximize a File
- Switch Between Files
- Close a File
- Using a SmartMaster

Tip

You can also use a SmartMaster to create a new file. SmartMasters save you time by providing the basic framework for many business and financial documents.

Note: For more information, refer to page 162.

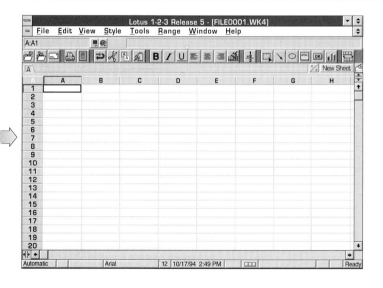

Think of each new file as a new 3-ring binder. A file can contain multiple worksheets. You can use these worksheets to organize related data.

◆ A new file appears.

Note: The previous file is now hidden behind the new file.

CASCADE FILES · TILE FILES

If you have several files open, some of them may be hidden from view. You can use the Cascade or Tile feature to view the contents of each file.

CASCADE FILES

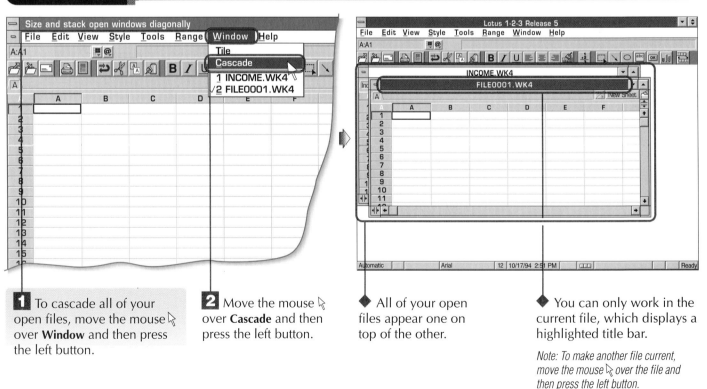

1 To cascade all of your open files, move the mouse over **Window** and then press the left button.

2 Move the mouse over **Cascade** and then press the left button.

◆ All of your open files appear one on top of the other.

◆ You can only work in the current file, which displays a highlighted title bar.

Note: To make another file current, move the mouse over the file and then press the left button.

156

Change Your Screen Display	Using Multiple Worksheets	**Using Multiple Files**	Charting Data	Drawing Objects	Working With Databases

- Create a New File
- **Cascade Files**
- **Tile Files**
- Maximize a File
- Switch Between Files
- Close a File
- Using a SmartMaster

You can easily copy or move data between tiled files displayed on your screen.

Note: For more information, refer to page 144.

TILE FILES

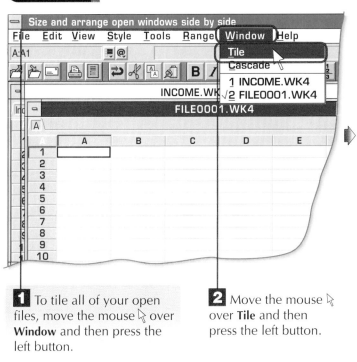

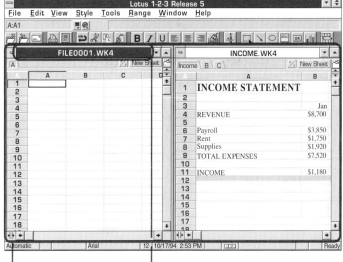

1 To tile all of your open files, move the mouse ⬀ over **Window** and then press the left button.

2 Move the mouse ⬀ over **Tile** and then press the left button.

◆ All of your open files appear side by side on your screen.

◆ You can only work in the current file, which displays a highlighted title bar.

Note: To make another file current, move the mouse ⬀ over the file and then press the left button.

MAXIMIZE A FILE
SWITCH BETWEEN FILES

You can enlarge a file to fill your screen. This lets you view more of its contents.

MAXIMIZE A FILE

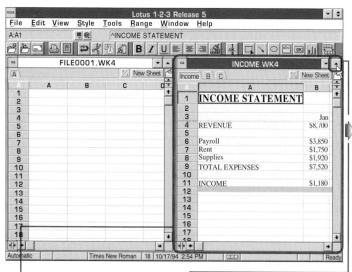

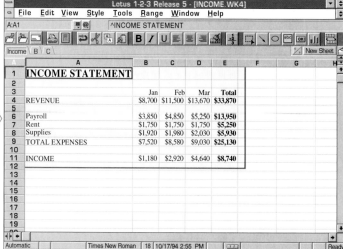

1 To select the file you want to maximize, move the mouse ⤢ anywhere over the file and then press the left button.

2 Move the mouse ⤢ over ▲ on the file you want to maximize and then press the left button.

◆ The file enlarges to fill your screen.

Note: The file covers all of your other open files.

Change Your Screen Display	Using Multiple Worksheets	Using Multiple Files	Charting Data	Drawing Objects	Working With Databases

- Create a New File
- Cascade Files
- Tile Files
- **Maximize a File**
- **Switch Between Files**
- Close a File
- Using a SmartMaster

You can easily switch between all of your open files. This lets you view the contents of each file.

SWITCH BETWEEN FILES

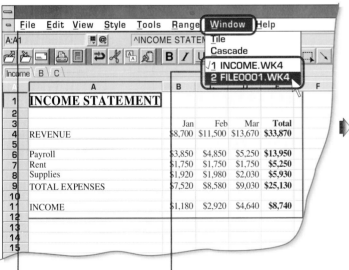

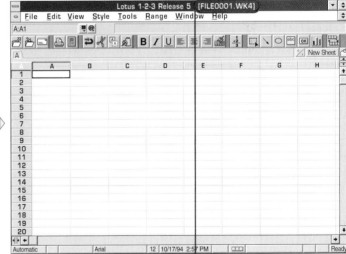

1 Move the mouse ⇖ over **Window** and then press the left button.

◆ A list of all your open files appears. The current file displays a check mark (√) beside its name.

2 Move the mouse ⇖ over the file you want to view and then press the left button.

◆ The file appears.

◆ The name of the file appears at the top of your screen.

When you finish working with a file, you can close the file to remove it from your screen.

CLOSE A FILE

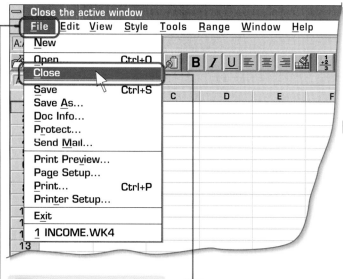

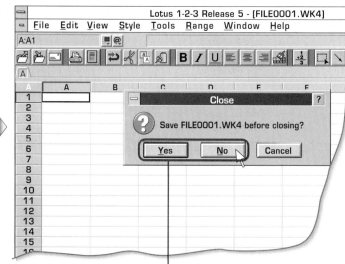

1 To close the file displayed on your screen, move the mouse ⬚ over **File** and then press the left button.

2 Move the mouse ⬚ over **Close** and then press the left button.

◆ The **Close** dialog box appears if you have not saved changes made to your file.

3 To close the file without saving the changes, move the mouse ⬚ over **No** and then press the left button.

◆ To save the changes, move the mouse ⬚ over **Yes** and then press the left button.

Note: For more information on saving a file, refer to page 28.

Change Your Screen Display	Using Multiple Worksheets	Using Multiple Files	Charting Data	Drawing Objects	Working With Databases

- Create a New File
- Cascade Files
- Tile Files
- Maximize a File
- Switch Between Files
- **Close a File**
- Using a SmartMaster

Tip

The Close and Exit features perform different tasks.

CLOSE	EXIT
The Close feature removes a file from your screen. You can continue to use the 1-2-3 program.	The Exit feature shuts off the 1-2-3 program. You will return to the Program Manager window.

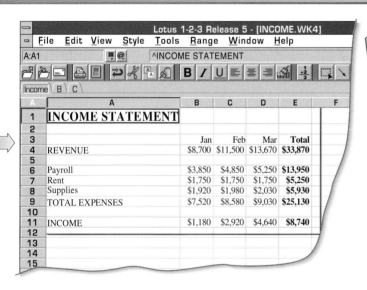

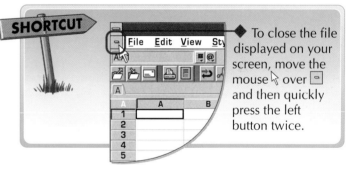

SHORTCUT

◆ To close the file displayed on your screen, move the mouse over ⊟ and then quickly press the left button twice.

◆ The file disappears from your screen.

Note: If you had more than one file open, the second last file you worked on appears.

USING A SMARTMASTER

> SmartMasters save you time by providing the basic framework for many commonly used business and financial documents.

USING A SMARTMASTER

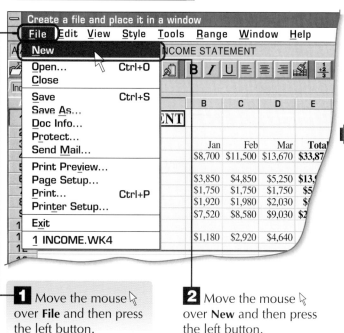

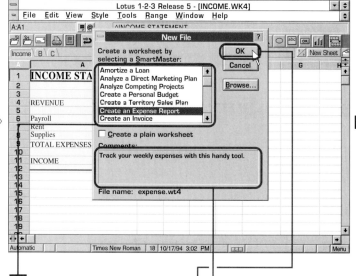

◆ This area displays a description of the highlighted SmartMaster.

1 Move the mouse over **File** and then press the left button.

2 Move the mouse over **New** and then press the left button.

◆ The **New File** dialog box appears.

3 Move the mouse over the SmartMaster you want to use and then press the left button.

Note: To view all of the available SmartMasters, use the scroll bar. For more information, refer to page 21.

4 Move the mouse over **OK** and then press the left button.

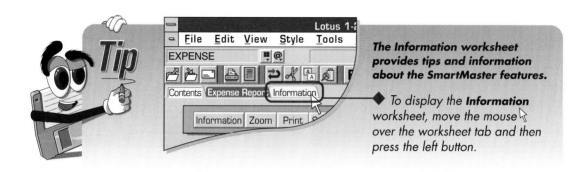

**The Information worksheet
provides tips and information
about the SmartMaster features.**

◆ To display the **Information**
worksheet, move the mouse
over the worksheet tab and then
press the left button.

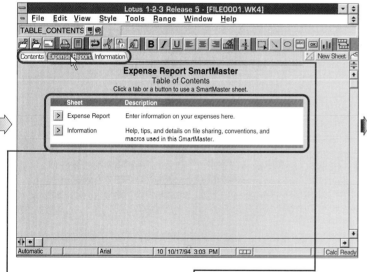

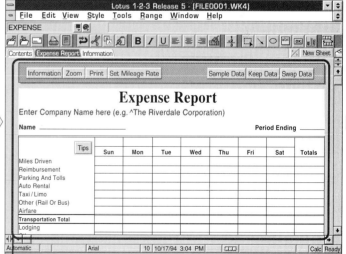

◆ The SmartMaster
appears displaying the
Contents worksheet.

◆ This area displays
a brief description of
the worksheets in the
SmartMaster you selected.

5 This SmartMaster contains
three worksheets. To display
another worksheet, move the
mouse over the worksheet
tab (example: **Expense Report**)
and then press the left button.

◆ The worksheet appears.

Note: To enter data in the worksheet,
refer to the next page.

USING A SMARTMASTER

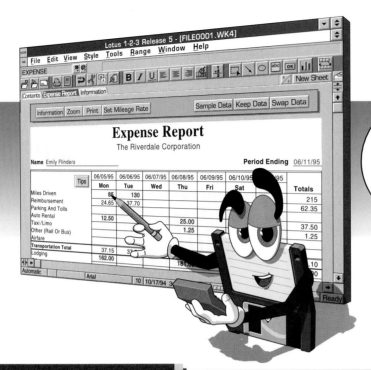

You can display sample data in a SmartMaster. This will show you where to enter data and where the results of calculations will appear.

USING A SMARTMASTER (CONTINUED)

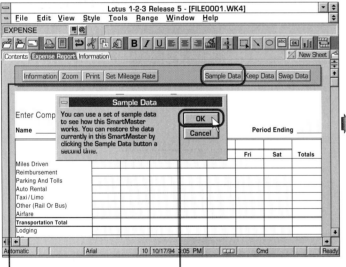

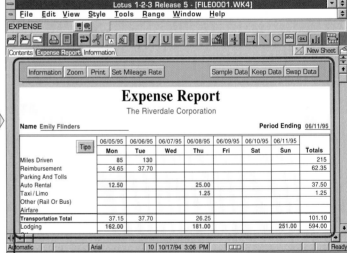

6 To display sample data in the worksheet, move the mouse over **Sample Data** and then press the left button.

◆ The **Sample Data** dialog box appears.

7 Move the mouse over **OK** and then press the left button.

◆ Sample data appears in the worksheet.

8 To hide the sample data, repeat steps **6** and **7**.

| Change Your Screen Display | Using Multiple Worksheets | **Using Multiple Files** | Charting Data | Drawing Objects | Working With Databases |

• Create a New File
• Cascade Files
• Tile Files
• Maximize a File
• Switch Between Files
• Close a File
• **Using a SmartMaster**

You can save and close a SmartMaster as you would any 1-2-3 file.

Note: To save a file, refer to page 28.
To close a file, refer to page 160.

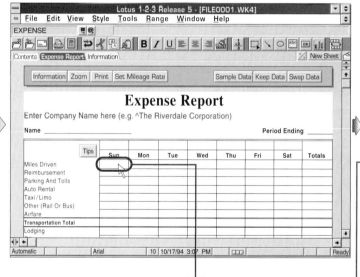

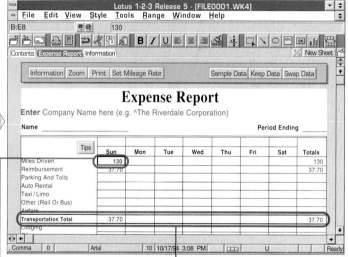

◆ You enter data into the yellow areas of the worksheet.

9 To enter data, move the mouse ▷ over a yellow area and then press the left button.

10 Type the data and then press **Enter** on your keyboard.

◆ A SmartMaster contains built-in formulas that perform calculations on the data you enter.

◆ For example, this row displays the transportation total for each day of the week.

verview

CHARTING DATA

◆ In this chapter you will learn how to create, change and print a chart. You will also learn how to create a map.

INTRODUCTION

You can use a chart to visually display your worksheet data. 1-2-3 offers many different chart types.

PARTS OF A CHART

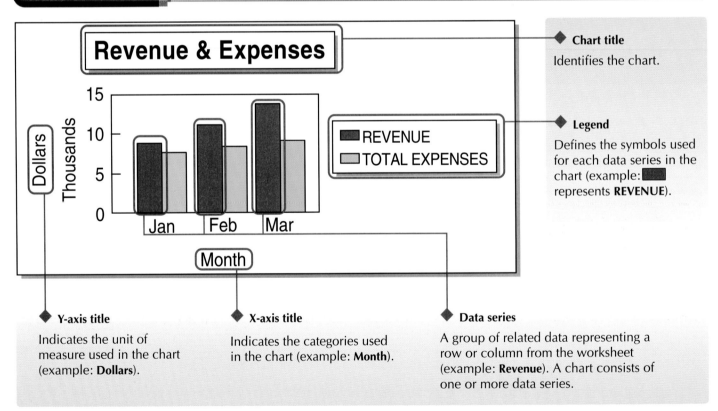

Chart title

Identifies the chart.

Legend

Defines the symbols used for each data series in the chart (example: ▨ represents **REVENUE**).

Y-axis title

Indicates the unit of measure used in the chart (example: **Dollars**).

X-axis title

Indicates the categories used in the chart (example: **Month**).

Data series

A group of related data representing a row or column from the worksheet (example: **Revenue**). A chart consists of one or more data series.

WORKING WITH LOTUS 1-2-3

Change Your Screen Display   Using Multiple Worksheets   Using Multiple Files   **Charting Data**   Drawing Objects   Working With Databases

- **Introduction**
- Create a Chart
- Move a Chart
- Size a Chart
- Change Chart Titles

- Change Chart Type
- Change Chart Colors
- Print a Chart
- Create a Map

CHART TYPES

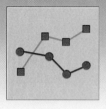

LINE

Each line represents a data series. This is useful for showing the rate of change in values over time (example: sales figures for the last five years).

AREA

Each line represents a data series. The area below each line is filled in. This is useful for showing the amount of change in values over time.

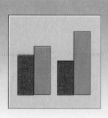

BAR

Each bar represents a value in a data series. This chart shows differences between values (example: a comparison of revenue and expenses for each month in a year).

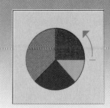

PIE

This chart shows each value in a data series as a piece of a pie. A pie chart can only display one data series at a time. This is useful for showing percentages (example: January sales as a percentage of sales for the year).

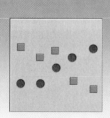

XY

This chart shows the relationship between two or more data series (example: relationship between education and lifetime earnings).

HLCO

A High-Low-Close-Open chart shows the range of values for a series of data. This chart is useful for showing data that fluctuates over a specific time period (example: stock market data).

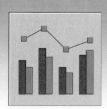

MIXED

This chart is a combination of a bar chart and a line or area chart (example: a line represents total company earnings and bars show departmental earnings).

RADAR

This chart represents each data series as a line around a central point (example: each month is an axis, the distance from the center point shows the sales for the month).

CREATE A CHART

You can create a chart directly from your worksheet data.

CREATE A CHART

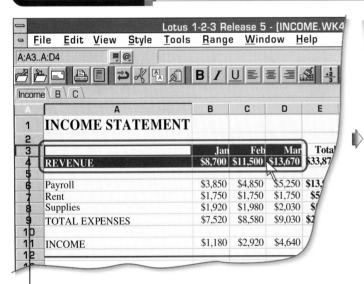

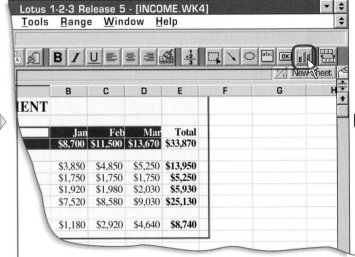

1 Select the cells containing the data you want to chart, including the row and column titles.

Note: To select cells, refer to page 14.

2 Move the mouse over 📊 and then press the left button.

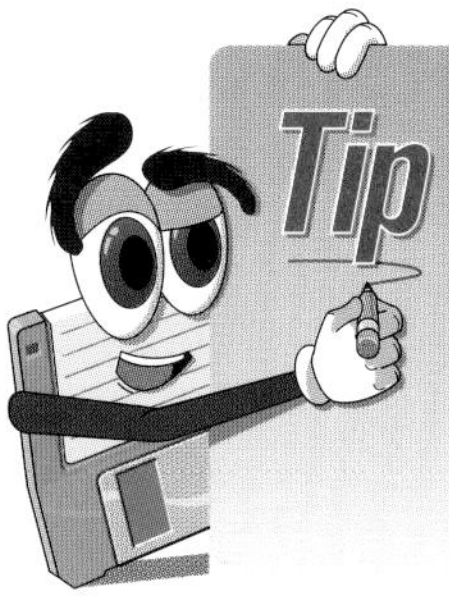

If you make changes to data in your worksheet, 1-2-3 will automatically update the chart to reflect the changes.

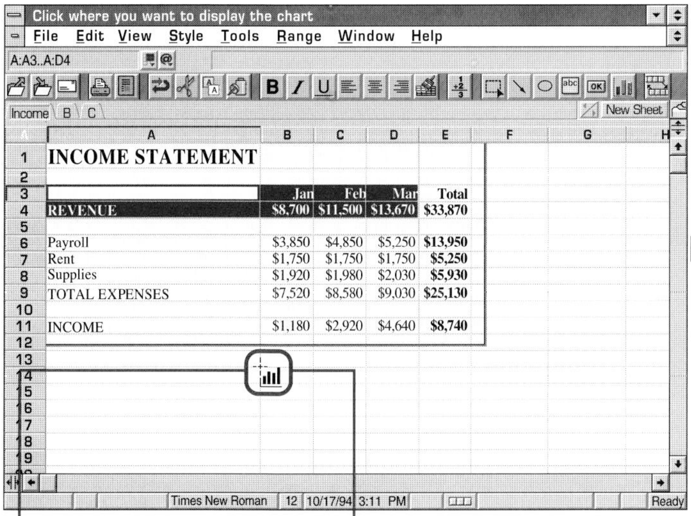

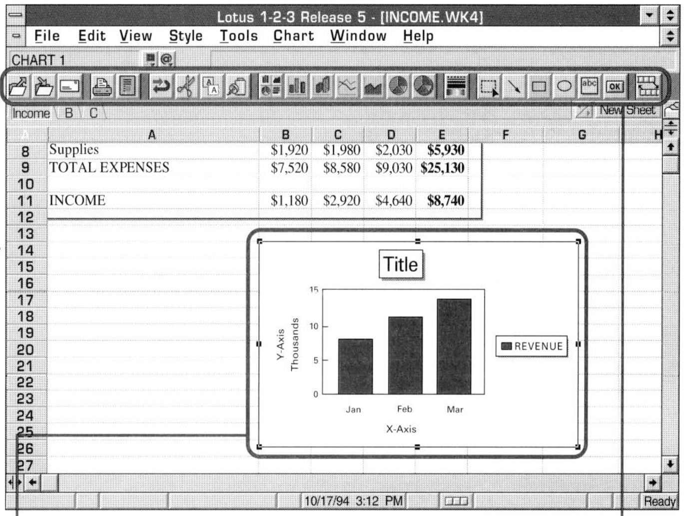

3 Move the mouse over your worksheet and changes to .

4 Move the mouse over the location where you want the top left corner of the chart to appear and then press the left button.

◆ The chart appears.

Note: To view the entire chart, use the scroll bar. For more information, refer to page 21.

◆ 1-2-3 displays the chart SmartIcons at the top of your screen.

MOVE A CHART SIZE A CHART

> After you create a chart, you can move it to a more suitable location in your worksheet. You can also change the overall size of a chart.

MOVE A CHART

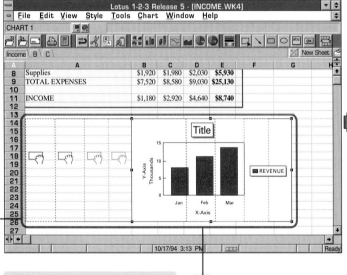

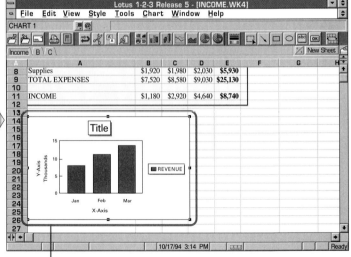

1 To move a chart, move the mouse ⬚ over an edge of the chart (not a handle ■).

2 Press and hold down the left button as you drag the chart to a new location.

◆ A dotted box indicates the new location.

3 Release the button and the chart moves to the new location.

Change Your Screen Display	Using Multiple Worksheets	Using Multiple Files	**Charting Data**	Drawing Objects	Working With Databases

Charting Data

- Introduction
- Create a Chart
- **Move a Chart**
- **Size a Chart**
- Change Chart Titles

- Change Chart Type
- Change Chart Colors
- Print a Chart
- Create a Map

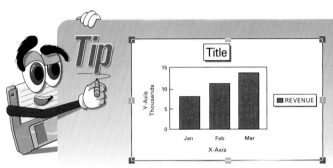

You can change the size of a chart using any handle around the chart.

You can use these handles to change the height of a chart.

You can use these handles to change the width of a chart.

You can use these handles to change the height and width of a chart at the same time.

SIZE A CHART

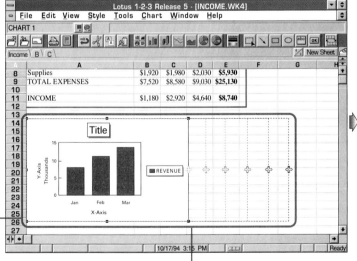

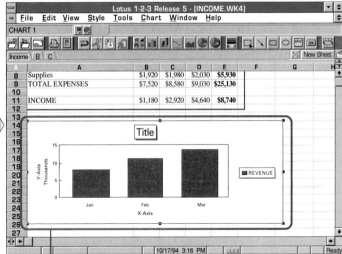

1 Move the mouse over an edge of the chart and then press the left button. Handles (■) appear around the chart.

2 Move the mouse over one of the handles (■) and ⬉ changes to ✛.

3 Press and hold down the left button as you drag the chart to a new size.

◆ A dotted box indicates the new size.

4 Release the button and the chart displays the new size.

CHANGE CHART TITLES

You can change the titles in your chart to make the chart more meaningful.

CHANGE CHART TITLES

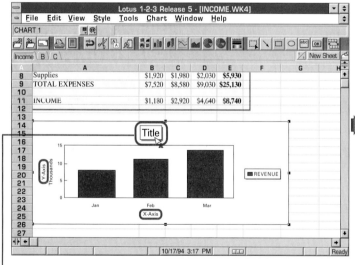

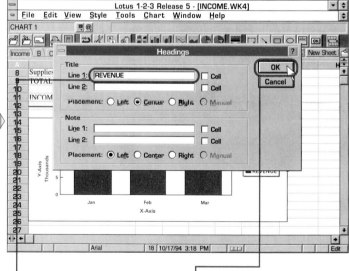

1 Move the mouse over the title you want to change and then quickly press the left button twice.

◆ A dialog box appears.

Note: The dialog box that appears depends on the title you selected in step **1**.

2 Type the new title (example: **REVENUE**).

3 Move the mouse over **OK** and then press the left button.

174

Tip

You can change the design and size of titles in a chart as you would change data in your worksheet.

1 Move the mouse over the title you want to change and then press the left button. Handles (■) appear around the title.

2 Perform steps **2** to **7** starting on page 90.

DELETE CHART TITLES

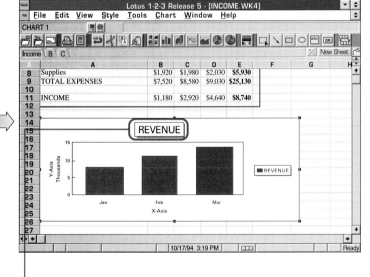

◆ The chart displays the new title.

Note: To deselect the title, move the mouse outside the title area and then press the left button.

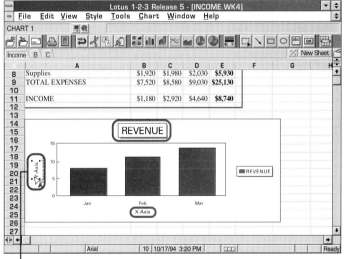

1 Move the mouse over the title you want to delete (example: **Y-Axis**) and then press the left button. Handles (■) appear around the title.

2 Press **Delete** on your keyboard.

CHANGE CHART TYPE

After creating a chart, you can select a new chart type that will better suit your data.

CHANGE CHART TYPE

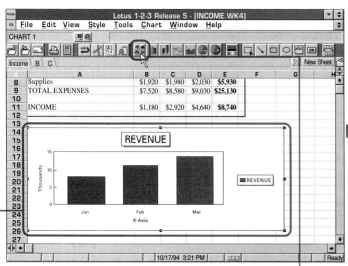

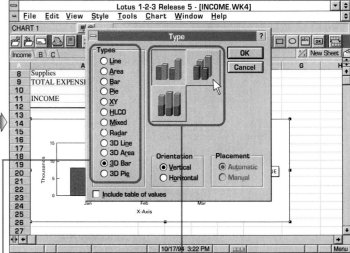

1 To select the chart you want to change, move the mouse ℞ over the chart and then press the left button.

2 Move the mouse ℞ over ▓▓ and then press the left button.

◆ The **Type** dialog box appears.

3 Move the mouse ℞ over the chart type you want to use (example: **3D Bar**) and then press the left button. ○ changes to ◉.

◆ The styles for the chart type you selected appear.

4 Move the mouse ℞ over the style you want to use and then press the left button.

Change Your Screen Display	Using Multiple Worksheets	Using Multiple Files	Charting Data	Drawing Objects	Working With Databases

Charting Data

- Introduction
- Create a Chart
- Move a Chart
- Size a Chart
- Change Chart Titles

- **Change Chart Type**
- Change Chart Colors
- Print a Chart
- Create a Map

SHORTCUT

To quickly change the chart type:

1 Move the mouse ⩗ over the chart you want to change and then press the left button.

2 Move the mouse ⩗ over one of the following SmartIcons and then press the left button.

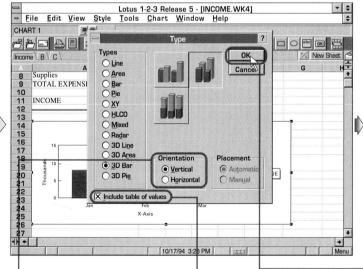

5 Move the mouse ⩗ over the orientation you want to use (example: **Vertical**) and then press the left button.

Note: You cannot change the orientation of a pie or radar chart.

6 To display the data used to create the chart below the chart, move the mouse ⩗ over this option and then press the left button (☐ changes to ☒).

Note: The table of values option is not available for all chart types.

7 Move the mouse ⩗ over **OK** and then press the left button.

◆ The new chart type appears.

◆ If you selected the table of values option in step **6**, the data used to create the chart appears.

177

CHANGE CHART COLORS

You can change the color of any part of your chart. Different colors can make your chart more attractive.

CHANGE CHART COLORS

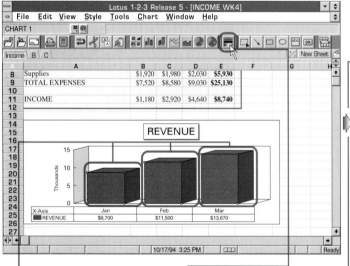

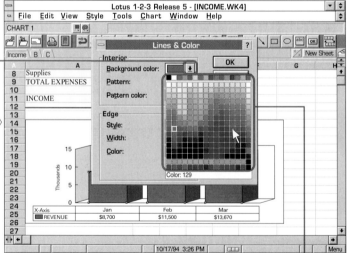

1 Move the mouse ⟋ over an edge of the area you want to display a new color and then press the left button. Handles (■) appear around the area.

2 Move the mouse ⟍ over ▤ and then press the left button.

◆ The **Lines & Color** dialog box appears.

3 Move the mouse ⟍ over ⬇ beside **Background color:** and then press the left button.

4 Move the mouse ⟍ over the color you want to use and then press the left button.

DELETE A CHART

1 Move the mouse over an edge of the chart you want to delete and then press the left button. Handles (■) appear around the chart.

2 Press Delete on your keyboard.

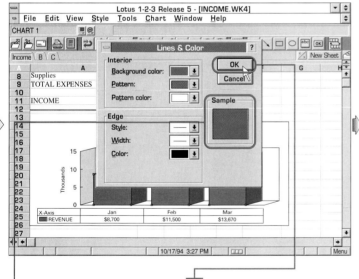

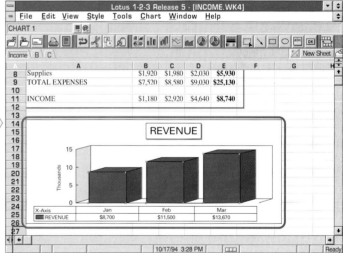

◆ This area displays a sample of the color you selected.

5 Move the mouse over **OK** and then press the left button.

◆ The chart displays the new color.

PRINT A CHART

You can print your chart on its own page or with the worksheet data.

PRINT A CHART ON ITS OWN PAGE

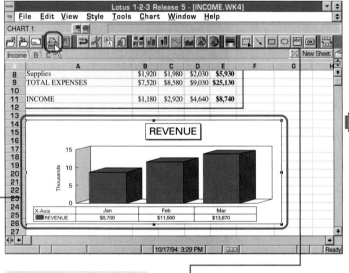

1 To print a chart on its own page, move the mouse over the chart and then press the left button.

2 Move the mouse over 🖨 and then press the left button.

◆ The **Print** dialog box appears.

3 Move the mouse over **Selected chart:** and then press the left button (○ changes to ◉).

4 Move the mouse over **OK** and then press the left button.

| Change Your Screen Display | Using Multiple Worksheets | Using Multiple Files | Charting Data | Drawing Objects | Working With Databases |

Charting Data

- Introduction
- Create a Chart
- Move a Chart
- Size a Chart
- Change Chart Titles
- Change Chart Type
- Change Chart Colors
- **Print a Chart**
- Create a Map

Tip

You can increase the size of a printed chart to fill a page.

1 Move the mouse over the chart you want to change and then press the left button.

2 Perform steps **1** to **5** starting on page 120, selecting **Fill page** in step **4**.

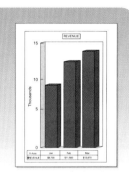

PRINT A CHART WITH THE WORKSHEET DATA

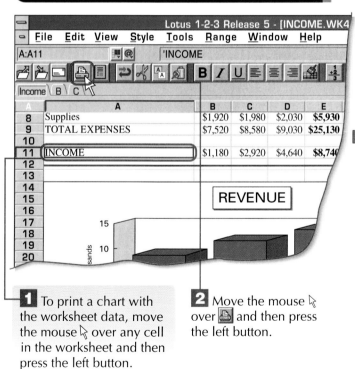

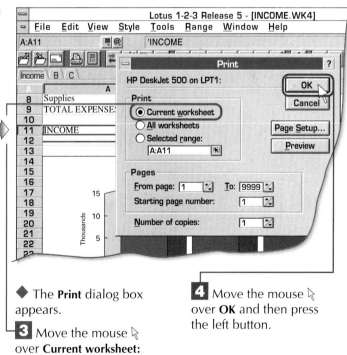

1 To print a chart with the worksheet data, move the mouse over any cell in the worksheet and then press the left button.

2 Move the mouse over 🖨 and then press the left button.

◆ The **Print** dialog box appears.

3 Move the mouse over **Current worksheet:** and then press the left button (○ changes to ◉).

4 Move the mouse over **OK** and then press the left button.

CREATE A MAP

USA by State

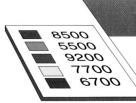

8500
5500
9200
7700
6700

CREATE A MAP

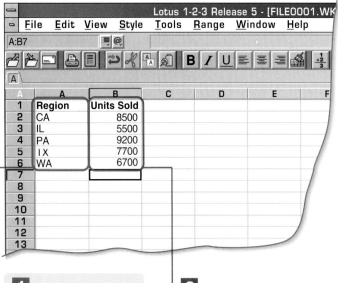

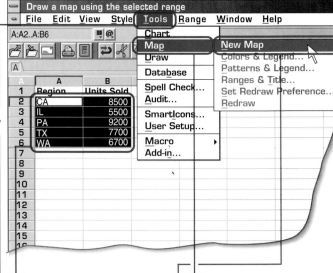

1 Enter the names of the regions or map codes (example: **Texas** or **TX**) in one column.

Note: This example adds a map to a new file. To create a new file, refer to page 154.

2 Enter the data for each region in the next column.

3 Select the cells containing the data you want to map.

4 Move the mouse ⊳ over **Tools** and then press the left button.

5 Move the mouse ⊳ over **Map** and then press the left button.

6 Move the mouse ⊳ over **New Map** and then press the left button.

Change Your Screen Display	Using Multiple Worksheets	Using Multiple Files	Charting Data	Drawing Objects	Working With Databases

Charting Data

- Introduction
- Create a Chart
- Move a Chart
- Size a Chart
- Change Chart Titles
- Change Chart Type
- Change Chart Colors
- Print a Chart
- **Create a Map**

1-2-3 will automatically create a map that corresponds to the region you enter in your worksheet. 1-2-3 provides maps for the following locations:

Alaska	Japan by Prefecture
Australia by State	Mexico by Estado
Canada by Province	Taiwan
Europe by Country	USA by State
European Union by Region	World Countries
Hawaii	

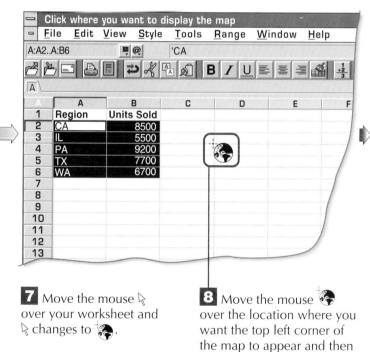

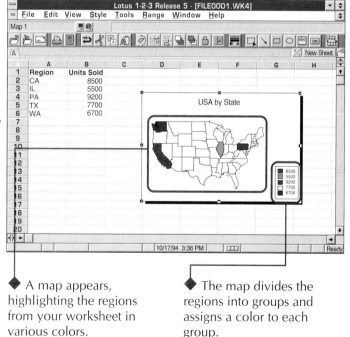

7 Move the mouse ▷ over your worksheet and ▷ changes to 🌐.

8 Move the mouse 🌐 over the location where you want the top left corner of the map to appear and then press the left button.

◆ A map appears, highlighting the regions from your worksheet in various colors.

◆ The map divides the regions into groups and assigns a color to each group.

183

DRAWING OBJECTS

Add a Text Block

Draw Shapes and Lines

Size an Object

Move an Object

◆ In this chapter you will learn how to emphasize data by adding objects to your worksheet.

ADD A TEXT BLOCK

You can add
a text block to
your worksheet to
provide additional
information about
your data.

ADD A TEXT BLOCK

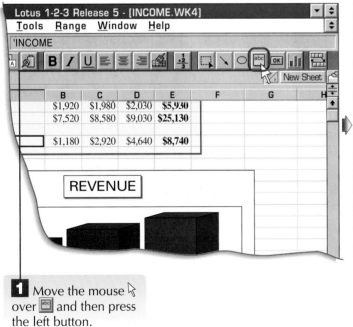

1 Move the mouse ↳ over [abc] and then press the left button.

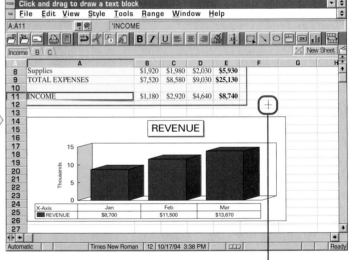

2 Move the mouse ↳ over your worksheet and ↳ changes to +.

3 Move the mouse + over the area where you want to display the top left corner of the text block.

WORKING WITH LOTUS 1-2-3

| Change Your Screen Display | Using Multiple Worksheets | Using Multiple Files | Charting Data | **Drawing Objects** | Working With Databases |

DELETE A TEXT BLOCK

1 To select the text block you want to delete, move the mouse I over the text block and then press the left button. Handles (■) appear around the text block.

2 Press **Delete** on your keyboard.

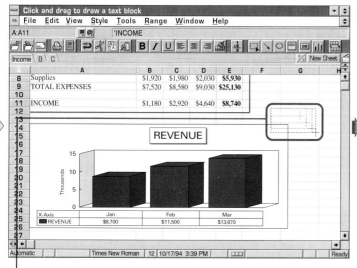

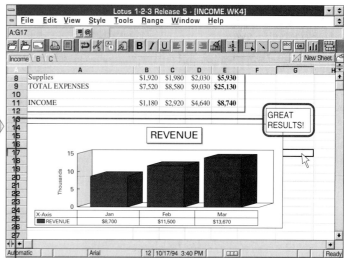

4 Press and hold down the left button as you drag the mouse + until the block displays the desired shape and size. Then release the button.

5 Type the text you want to appear in the text block.

6 When you finish typing the text, move the mouse ↖ outside the text block and then press the left button.

DRAW SHAPES AND LINES

You can draw shapes and lines to emphasize specific areas in your worksheet.

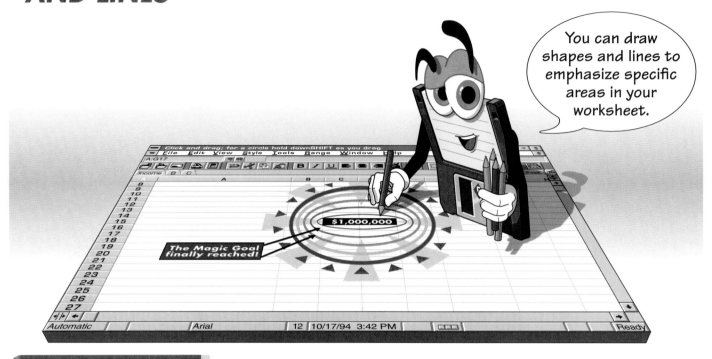

DRAW SHAPES AND LINES

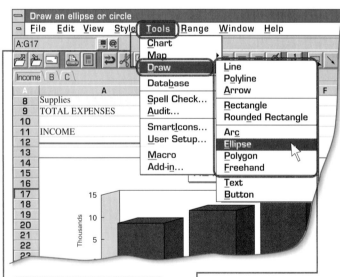

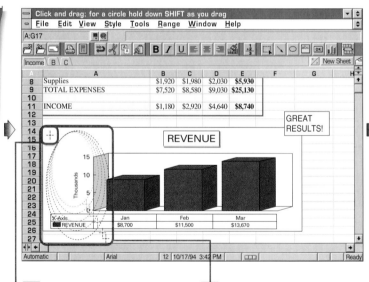

1 Move the mouse over **Tools** and then press the left button.

2 Move the mouse over **Draw** and then press the left button.

3 Move the mouse over the shape or line you want to draw and then press the left button.

4 Move the mouse over your worksheet and ⌖ changes to +.

5 Move the mouse + over the area where you want to begin drawing the shape or line.

6 Press and hold down the left button as you drag the mouse + until the shape or line displays the desired size. Then release the button.

188

Change
Your Screen
Display

Using
Multiple
Worksheets

Using
Multiple Files

Charting
Data

**Drawing
Objects**

Working With
Databases

• Add a Text Block
• **Draw Shapes and Lines**
• Size an Object
• Move an Object

DELETE A SHAPE OR LINE

1 Move the mouse ▷ over an edge of the object you want to delete and then press the left button. Handles (■) appear around the object.

2 Press **Delete** on your keyboard.

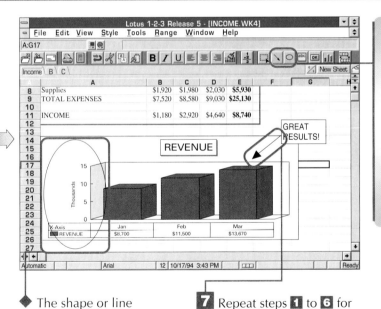

You can use these SmartIcons to quickly draw an arrow or circle in your worksheet.

1 To create an arrow, move the mouse ▷ over ↘ and then press the left button.

◆ To create a circle, move the mouse ▷ over ○ and then press the left button.

2 To draw the arrow or circle, perform steps **5** and **6** on page 188.

◆ The shape or line appears.

7 Repeat steps **1** to **6** for each shape or line you want to draw.

Note: To deselect an object, move the mouse ▷ outside the object and then press the left button.

SIZE AN MOVE AN
OBJECT OBJECT

> You can easily change the size or location of an object in your worksheet.

SIZE AN OBJECT

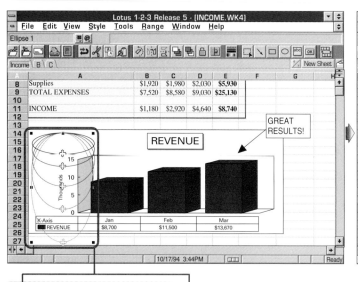

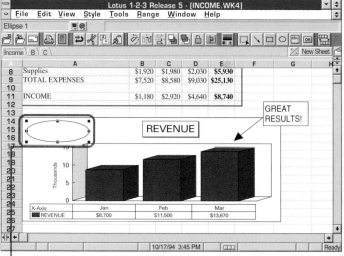

1 To select the object you want to size, move the mouse over an edge of the object and then press the left button. Handles (■) appear around the object.

2 Move the mouse over one of the handles (changes to) and then press and hold down the left button.

3 Still holding down the left button, drag the mouse until the object displays the desired size.

4 Release the button and the object displays the new size.

190

Change Your Screen Display	Using Multiple Worksheets	Using Multiple Files	Charting Data	Drawing Objects	Working With Databases

- Add a Text Block
- Draw Shapes and Lines
- **Size an Object**
- **Move an Object**

You can change the size of an object using the handles around the object.

You can use these handles to change the height of an object.

You can use these handles to change the width of an object.

You can use these handles to change the height and width of an object at the same time.

MOVE AN OBJECT

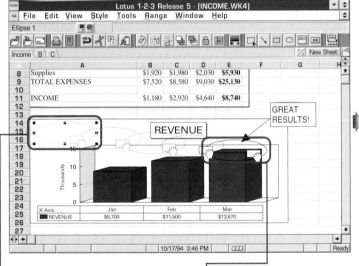

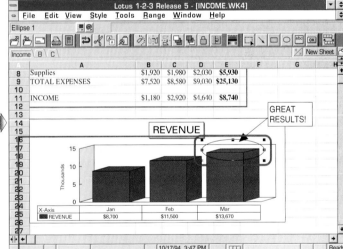

1 Move the mouse ↳ over an edge (not a handle ■) of the object you want to move and then press and hold down the left button.

2 Still holding down the left button, drag the mouse ☜ where you want to place the object.

3 Release the button and the object appears in the new location.

verview

WORKING WITH DATABASES

Introduction

Create a Database

Find Records

Sort Data

Extract Records

◆ In this chapter you will learn how to find, sort and extract data from a large collection of information.

1-2-3 provides powerful tools for organizing, managing, sorting and retrieving data from a large collection of information.

WORKING WITH LOTUS 1-2-3

Change Your Screen Display	Using Multiple Worksheets	Using Multiple Files	Charting Data	Drawing Objects	Working With Databases

- **Introduction**
- Create a Database
- Find Records
- Sort Data
- Extract Records

STORE DATA

You can keep your data in an organized and up-to-date list. For example, you can create a database to keep track of the number of units each employee sells every month.

SORT DATA

You can change the order that data appears in a database. 1-2-3 lets you sort data by letter or number. For example, you can alphabetically sort the names of all your employees.

FIND DATA

You can easily find specific data in a large database. You can then compare and analyze the data. For example, you can search for the names of all employees who sold more than 1000 units last month.

CREATE A DATABASE

You can create a database in a worksheet to store a collection of related data.

RECORDS

A record is a group of related data in a database (example: all the information for one employee).

FIELD NAMES

A field name is a title for one category of data in a record (example: **Last Name**).

CREATE A DATABASE

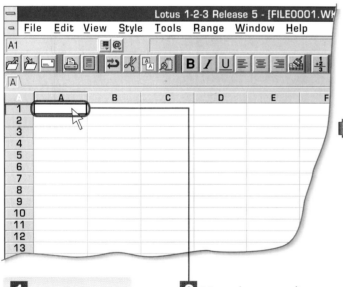

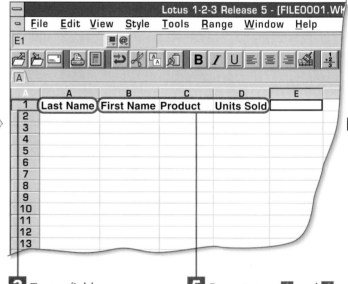

1 Create a new file.

Note: To create a new file, refer to page 154.

2 Move the mouse ⊳ over the cell where you want to begin the database (example: **A1**) and then press the left button.

3 Type a field name (example: **Last Name**).

4 Press → on your keyboard to enter the field name and move to the next cell.

5 Repeat steps **3** and **4** until you have entered all the field names.

Note: To bold the field names, refer to page 86. To change the column width, refer to page 76.

WORKING WITH LOTUS 1-2-3

| Change Your Screen Display | Using Multiple Worksheets | Using Multiple Files | Charting Data | Drawing Objects | **Working With Databases** |

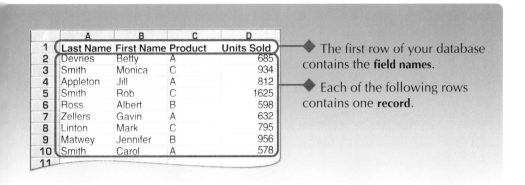

	A	B	C	D
1	**Last Name**	**First Name**	**Product**	**Units Sold**
2	Devries	Betty	A	685
3	Smith	Monica	C	934
4	Appleton	Jill	A	812
5	Smith	Rob	C	1625
6	Ross	Albert	B	598
7	Zellers	Gavin	A	632
8	Linton	Mark	C	795
9	Matwey	Jennifer	B	956
10	Smith	Carol	A	578
11				

◆ The first row of your database contains the **field names**.

◆ Each of the following rows contains one **record**.

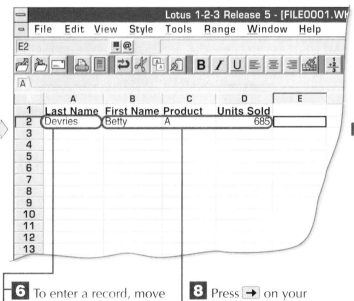

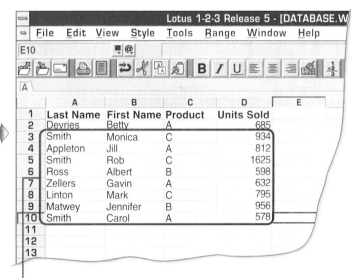

6 To enter a record, move the mouse � over the empty cell below the first field name (example: **A2**) and then press the left button.

7 Type the data that corresponds to the field name (example: **Devries**).

8 Press → on your keyboard to enter the data and move to the next cell.

9 Repeat steps **7** and **8** until you have entered all the data for the record.

10 Repeat steps **6** to **9** until you have entered the data for all your records.

Note: Do not leave blank rows between your records.

11 Save your database to store it for future use.

Note: For more information on saving a file, refer to page 28.

FIND RECORDS

You can search for specific records in your database. When 1-2-3 completes the search, it highlights all matching records.

FIND RECORDS

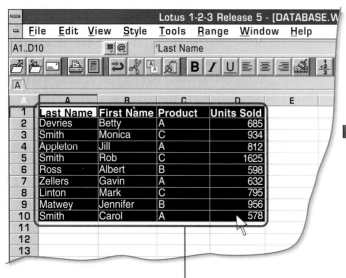

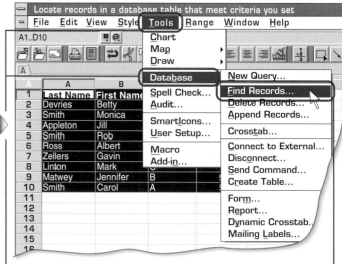

In this example, 1-2-3 will find all employees with the last name Smith who sell product C.

1 Select the cells containing the database, including the field names.

Note: To select cells, refer to page 14.

2 Move the mouse over **Tools** and then press the left button.

3 Move the mouse over **Database** and then press the left button.

4 Move the mouse over **Find Records** and then press the left button.

WORKING WITH LOTUS 1-2-3

Change Your Screen Display   Using Multiple Worksheets   Using Multiple Files   Charting Data   Drawing Objects   **Working With Databases**

- Introduction
- Create a Database
- **Find Records**
- Sort Data
- Extract Records

OPERATORS

=	finds all records that match
<	finds all records that are lower
>	finds all records that are higher
<=	finds all records that match or are lower
>=	finds all records that match or are higher
<>	finds all records that do not match

Note: 1 is lower than 2; A is lower than B.

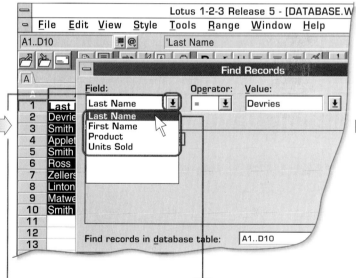

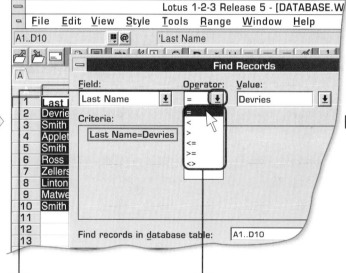

◆ The **Find Records** dialog box appears.

5 To display a list of field names from your database, move the mouse ▷ over ⬇ below **Field:** and then press the left button.

6 Move the mouse ▷ over the field name for the data you want to base the search on (example: **Last Name**) and then press the left button.

7 To display a list of operators, move the mouse ▷ over ⬇ below **Operator:** and then press the left button.

8 Move the mouse ▷ over the operator you want to use (example: =) and then press the left button.

To continue, refer to the next page.

FIND RECORDS

You must give 1-2-3 instructions to indicate which records you want to find. Each instruction is called a criterion.

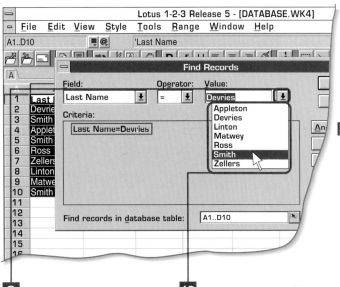

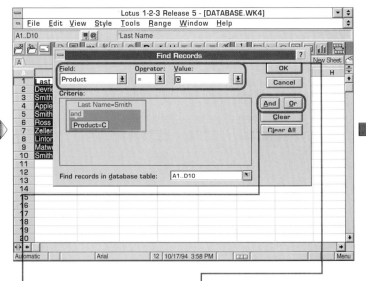

9 To display a list of values from your database, move the mouse ⟨ over ⬇ below **Value:** and then press the left button.

10 Move the mouse ⟨ over the value you want to base the search on (example: **Smith**) and then press the left button.

11 To add another criterion, move the mouse ⟨ over `And` or `Or` and then press the left button.

*Note: **And** narrows your search. **Or** expands your search. For more information, refer to the top of page 201.*

12 To specify the criterion, repeat steps **5** to **10**, starting on page 199.

WORKING WITH LOTUS 1-2-3

| Change Your Screen Display | Using Multiple Worksheets | Using Multiple Files | Charting Data | Drawing Objects | **Working With Databases** |

You can narrow or expand your search by using more than one criterion.

AND

And narrows your search by finding only the records that meet both criteria.

In the following example, 1-2-3 will highlight the records of all employees with the last name Smith who sell product C.

Criterion 1	And	Criterion 2
Last Name = Smith		Product = C

OR

Or expands your search by finding the records that meet one or both criteria.

In the following example, 1-2-3 will highlight the records of all employees with the last name Smith and all employees who sell product C.

Criterion 1	Or	Criterion 2
Last Name = Smith		Product = C

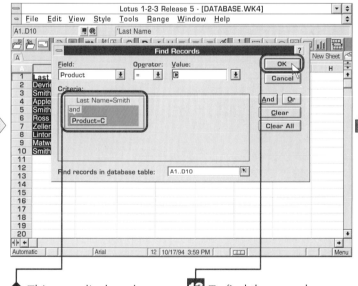

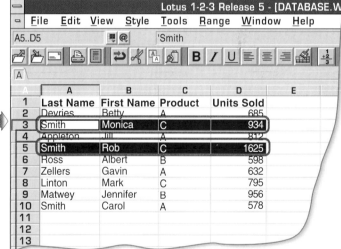

◆ This area displays the criteria you specified.

13 To find the records, move the mouse ⌖ over **OK** and then press the left button.

◆ 1-2-3 highlights all records matching the criteria you specified.

◆ To move through the matching records, press `Ctrl` + `Enter`.

Note: To deselect the cells, move the mouse ⌖ over any cell in the worksheet and then press the left button.

201

SORT DATA

You can use the Sort feature to change the order of records in your database.

SORT DATA

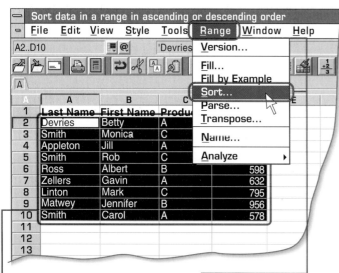

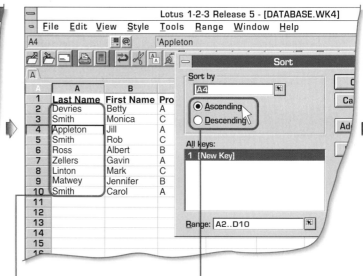

◆ The **Sort** dialog box appears.

1 Select the cells containing the data you want to sort. Do not select the field names, otherwise 1-2-3 will sort them with the data.

Note: To select cells, refer to page 14.

2 Move the mouse ⤢ over **Range** and then press the left button.

3 Move the mouse ⤢ over **Sort** and then press the left button.

4 To specify the column you want to sort, move the mouse 🖰 over any cell in the column (example: **column A**) and then press the left button.

5 Move the mouse ⤢ over the direction you want to sort the data and then press the left button (○ changes to ⦿).

*Note: **Ascending** sorts from A to Z, 0 to 9. **Descending** sorts from Z to A, 9 to 0.*

Change
Your Screen
Display

Using
Multiple
Worksheets

Using
Multiple Files

Charting
Data

Drawing
Objects

**Working With
Databases**

SECONDARY SORTS

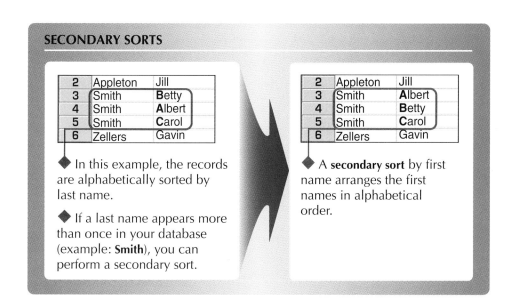

◆ In this example, the records are alphabetically sorted by last name.

◆ If a last name appears more than once in your database (example: **Smith**), you can perform a secondary sort.

◆ A **secondary sort** by first name arranges the first names in alphabetical order.

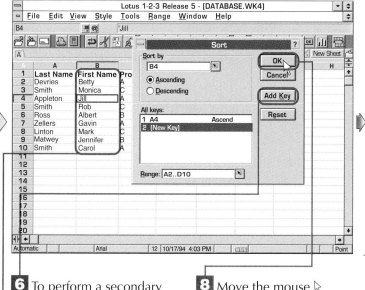

6 To perform a secondary sort, move the mouse ⇖ over **Add Key** and then press the left button.

7 Repeat steps **4** and **5** to specify the column you want to base the secondary sort on (example: **column B**).

8 Move the mouse ⇖ over **OK** and then press the left button.

◆ In this example, the last names are alphabetically sorted.

Note: To deselect cells, move the mouse ⇖ over any cell in the worksheet and then press the left button.

◆ All records with the same last name (example: **Smith**) are alphabetically sorted by first name.

EXTRACT RECORDS

You can search for records containing specific data and then copy these records to another area in your worksheet. This lets you easily compare data by displaying only the records you need.

EXTRACT RECORDS

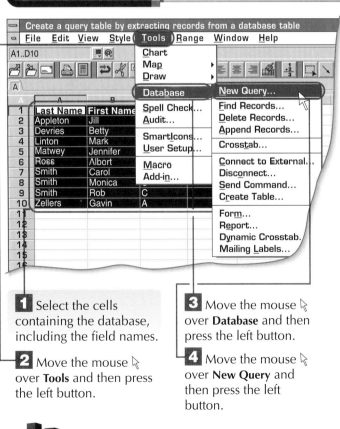

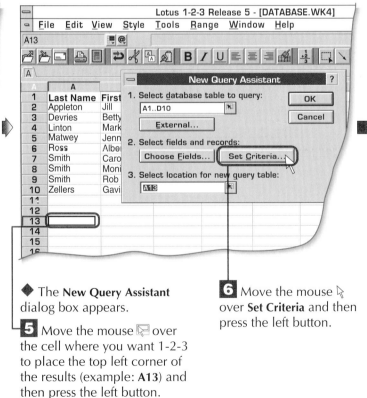

1 Select the cells containing the database, including the field names.

2 Move the mouse ⇗ over **Tools** and then press the left button.

3 Move the mouse ⇗ over **Database** and then press the left button.

4 Move the mouse ⇗ over **New Query** and then press the left button.

◆ The **New Query Assistant** dialog box appears.

5 Move the mouse ⇗ over the cell where you want 1-2-3 to place the top left corner of the results (example: **A13**) and then press the left button.

6 Move the mouse ⇗ over **Set Criteria** and then press the left button.

Change Your Screen Display	Using Multiple Worksheets	Using Multiple Files	Charting Data	Drawing Objects	**Working With Databases**

OPERATORS

=	finds all records that match
<	finds all records that are lower
>	finds all records that are higher
<=	finds all records that match or are lower
>=	finds all records that match or are higher
<>	finds all records that do not match

Note: 1 is lower than 2; A is lower than B.

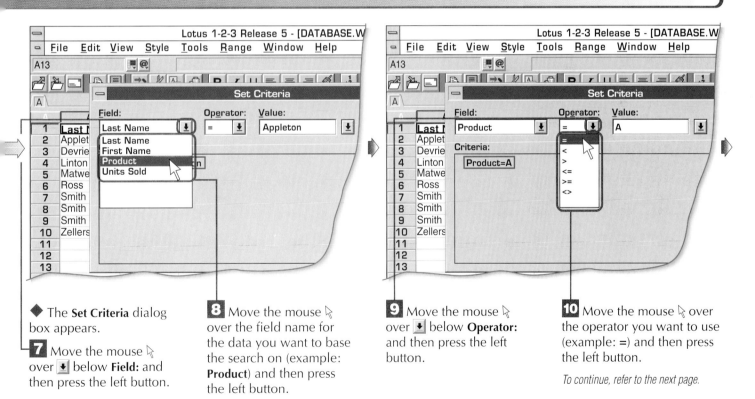

◆ The **Set Criteria** dialog box appears.

7 Move the mouse ▷ over ⬇ below **Field:** and then press the left button.

8 Move the mouse ▷ over the field name for the data you want to base the search on (example: **Product**) and then press the left button.

9 Move the mouse ▷ over ⬇ below **Operator:** and then press the left button.

10 Move the mouse ▷ over the operator you want to use (example: =) and then press the left button.

To continue, refer to the next page.

EXTRACT RECORDS

You must give 1-2-3 instructions to indicate which records you want to find. Each instruction is called a criterion.

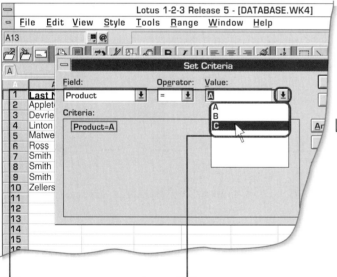

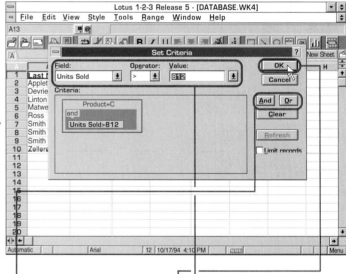

11 Move the mouse ⯆ over ⯆ below **Value:** and then press the left button.

12 Move the mouse ⯆ over the value you want to base the search on (example: **C**) and then press the left button.

13 To add another criterion, move the mouse ⯆ over And or Or and then press the left button.

*Note: **And** narrows your search. **Or** expands your search. For more information, refer to the top of page 207.*

14 To specify the criterion, repeat steps **7** to **12**, starting on page 205.

15 Move the mouse ⯆ over **OK** and then press the left button.

WORKING WITH LOTUS 1-2-3

| Change Your Screen Display | Using Multiple Worksheets | Using Multiple Files | Charting Data | Drawing Objects | Working With Databases |

You can narrow or expand your search by using more than one criterion.

AND

And narrows your search by extracting only the records that meet both criteria.

In the following example, 1-2-3 will extract the records of all employees selling product C who sold more than 812 units.

Criterion 1	**And**	Criterion 2
Product = C		Units Sold > 812

OR

Or expands your search by extracting the records that meet one or both criteria.

In the following example, 1-2-3 will extract the records of all employees selling product C and all employees who sold more than 812 units.

Criterion 1	**Or**	Criterion 2
Product = C		Units Sold > 812

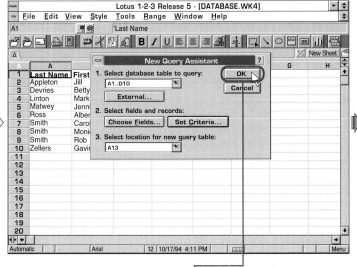

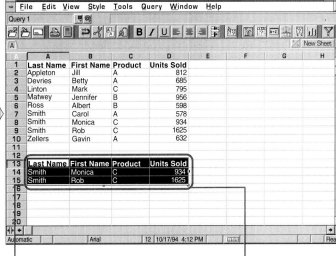

◆ The **New Query Assistant** dialog box reappears.

16 Move the mouse ⌖ over **OK** and then press the left button.

◆ A copy of each matching record appears in the location you specified.

DELETE THE RESULTS

1 Move the mouse ⌖ over an edge of the results and then press the left button. Handles (■) appear around the results.

2 Press `Delete`.

INDEX

Title	Author	ISBN #	Price
INTERNET/COMMUNICATIONS/NETWORKING			
CompuServe For Dummies™	by Wallace Wang	ISBN: 1-56884-181-7	$19.95 USA/$26.95 Canada
Modems For Dummies™, 2nd Edition	by Tina Rathbone	ISBN: 1-56884-223-6	$19.99 USA/$26.99 Canada
Modems For Dummies™	by Tina Rathbone	ISBN: 1-56884-001-2	$19.95 USA/$26.95 Canada
MORE Internet For Dummies™	by John Levine & Margaret Levine Young	ISBN: 1-56884-164-7	$19.95 USA/$26.95 Canada
NetWare For Dummies™	by Ed Tittel & Deni Connor	ISBN: 1-56884-003-9	$19.95 USA/$26.95 Canada
Networking For Dummies™	by Doug Lowe	ISBN: 1-56884-079-9	$19.95 USA/$26.95 Canada
ProComm Plus 2 For Windows For Dummies™	by Wallace Wang	ISBN: 1-56884-219-8	$19.99 USA/$26.99 Canada
The Internet Help Desk For Dummies™	by John Kaufeld	ISBN: 1-56884-238-4	$16.99 USA/$22.99 Canada
The3 Internet For Dummies™, 2nd Edition	by John Levine & Carol Baroudi	ISBN: 1-56884-222-8	$19.99 USA/$26.99 Canada
The Internet For Macs For Dummies™	by Charles Seiter	ISBN: 1-56884-184-1	$19.95 USA/$26.95 Canada
MACINTOSH			
Mac Programming For Dummies™	by Dan Parks Sydow	ISBN: 1-56884-173-6	$19.95 USA/$26.95 Canada
Macintosh System 7.5 For Dummies™	by Bob LeVitus	ISBN: 1-56884-197-3	$19.95 USA/$26.95 Canada
MORE Macs For Dummies™	by David Pogue	ISBN: 1-56884-087-X	$19.95 USA/$26.95 Canada
PageMaker 5 For Macs For Dummies™	by Galen Gruman & Deke McClelland	ISBN: 1-56884-178-7	$19.95 USA/$26.95 Canada
QuarkXPress 3.3 For Dummies™	by Galen Gruman & Barbara Assadi	ISBN: 1-56884-217-1	$19.99 USA/$26.99 Canada
Upgrading and Fixing Macs For Dummies™	by Kearney Rietmann & Frank Higgins	ISBN: 1-56884-189-2	$19.95 USA/$26.95 Canada
MULTIMEDIA			
Multimedia & CD-ROMs For Dummies™, Interactive Multimedia Value Pack	by Andy Rathbone	ISBN: 1-56884-225-2	$29.95 USA/$39.95 Canada
Multimedia & CD-ROMs For Dummies™	by Andy Rathbone	ISBN: 1-56884-089-6	$19.95 USA/$26.95 Canada
OPERATING SYSTEMS/DOS			
MORE DOS For Dummies™	by Dan Gookin	ISBN: 1-56884-046-2	$19.95 USA/$26.95 Canada
S.O.S. For DOS™	by Katherine Murray	ISBN: 1-56884-043-8	$12.95 USA/$16.95 Canada
OS/2 For Dummies™	by Andy Rathbone	ISBN: 1-878058-76-2	$19.95 USA/$26.95 Canada
UNIX			
UNIX For Dummies™	by John Levine & Margaret Levine Young	ISBN: 1-878058-58-4	$19.95 USA/$26.95 Canada
WINDOWS			
S.O.S. For Windows™	by Katherine Murray	ISBN: 1-56884-045-4	$12.95 USA/$16.95 Canada
Windows "X" For Dummies™, 3rd Edition	by Andy Rathbone	ISBN: 1-56884-240-6	$19.99 USA/$26.99 Canada
PCS/HARDWARE			
Illustrated Computer Dictionary For Dummies™	by Dan Gookin, Wally Wang, & Chris Van Buren	ISBN: 1-56884-004-7	$12.95 USA/$16.95 Canada
Upgrading and Fixing PCs For Dummies™	by Andy Rathbone	ISBN: 1-56884-002-0	$19.95 USA/$26.95 Canada
PRESENTATION/AUTOCAD			
AutoCAD For Dummies™	by Bud Smith	ISBN: 1-56884-191-4	$19.95 USA/$26.95 Canada
PowerPoint 4 For Windows For Dummies™	by Doug Lowe	ISBN: 1-56884-161-2	$16.95 USA/$22.95 Canada
PROGRAMMING			
Borland C++ For Dummies™	by Michael Hyman	ISBN: 1-56884-162-0	$19.95 USA/$26.95 Canada
"Borland's New Language Product" For Dummies™	by Neil Rubenking	ISBN: 1-56884-200-7	$19.95 USA/$26.95 Canada
C For Dummies™	by Dan Gookin	ISBN: 1-878058-78-9	$19.95 USA/$26.95 Canada
C++ For Dummies™	by S. Randy Davis	ISBN: 1-56884-163-9	$19.95 USA/$26.95 Canada
Mac Programming For Dummies™	by Dan Parks Sydow	ISBN: 1-56884-173-6	$19.95 USA/$26.95 Canada
QBasic Programming For Dummies™	by Douglas Hergert	ISBN: 1-56884-093-4	$19.95 USA/$26.95 Canada
Visual Basic "X" For Dummies™, 2nd Edition	by Wallace Wang	ISBN: 1-56884-230-9	$19.99 USA/$26.99 Canada
Visual Basic 3 For Dummies™	by Wallace Wang	ISBN: 1-56884-076-4	$19.95 USA/$26.95 Canada
SPREADSHEET			
1-2-3 For Dummies™	by Greg Harvey	ISBN: 1-878058-60-6	$16.95 USA/$22.95 Canada
1-2-3 For Windows 5 For Dummies™, 2nd Edition	by John Walkenbach	ISBN: 1-56884-216-3	$16.95 USA/$22.95 Canada
1-2-3 For Windows For Dummies™	by John Walkenbach	ISBN: 1-56884-052-7	$16.95 USA/$22.95 Canada
Excel 5 For Macs For Dummies™	by Greg Harvey	ISBN: 1-56884-186-8	$19.95 USA/$26.95 Canada
Excel For Dummies™, 2nd Edition	by Greg Harvey	ISBN: 1-56884-050-0	$16.95 USA/$22.95 Canada
MORE Excel 5 For Windows For Dummies™	by Greg Harvey	ISBN: 1-56884-207-4	$19.95 USA/$26.95 Canada
Quattro Pro 6 For Windows For Dummies™	by John Walkenbach	ISBN: 1-56884-174-4	$19.95 USA/$26.95 Canada
Quattro Pro For DOS For Dummies™	by John Walkenbach	ISBN: 1-56884-023-3	$16.95 USA/$22.95 Canada
UTILITIES			
Norton Utilities 8 For Dummies™	by Beth Slick	ISBN: 1-56884-166-3	$19.95 USA/$26.95 Canada
VCRS/CAMCORDERS			
VCRs & Camcorders For Dummies™	by Andy Rathbone & Gordon McComb	ISBN: 1-56884-229-5	$14.99 USA/$20.99 Canada
WORD PROCESSING			
Ami Pro For Dummies™	by Jim Meade	ISBN: 1-56884-049-7	$19.95 USA/$26.95 Canada
More Word For Windows 6 For Dummies™	by Doug Lowe	ISBN: 1-56884-165-5	$19.95 USA/$26.95 Canada
MORE WordPerfect 6 For Windows For Dummies™	by Margaret Levine Young & David C. Kay	ISBN: 1-56884-206-6	$19.95 USA/$26.95 Canada
MORE WordPerfect 6 For DOS For Dummies™	by Wallace Wang, edited by Dan Gookin	ISBN: 1-56884-047-0	$19.95 USA/$26.95 Canada
S.O.S. For WordPerfect™	by Katherine Murray	ISBN: 1-56884-053-5	$12.95 USA/$16.95 Canada
Word 6 For Macs For Dummies™	by Dan Gookin	ISBN: 1-56884-190-6	$19.95 USA/$26.95 Canada
Word For Windows 6 For Dummies™	by Dan Gookin	ISBN: 1-56884-075-6	$16.95 USA/$22.95 Canada
Word For Windows 2 For Dummies™	by Dan Gookin	ISBN: 1-878058-86-X	$16.95 USA/$22.95 Canada
WordPerfect 6 For Dummies™	by Dan Gookin	ISBN: 1-878058-77-0	$16.95 USA/$22.95 Canada
WordPerfect For Dummies™	by Dan Gookin	ISBN: 1-878058-52-5	$16.95 USA/$22.95 Canada
WordPerfect For Windows For Dummies™	by Margaret Levine Young & David C. Kay	ISBN: 1-56884-032-2	$16.95 USA/$22.95 Canada

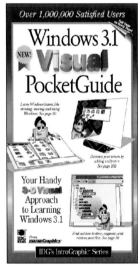

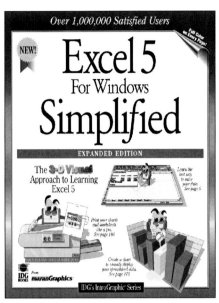
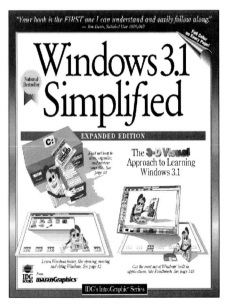

ORDER FORM

TRADE & INDIVIDUAL ORDERS

Phone: **(800) 762-2974** or **(317) 895-5200**
(8 a.m.–6 p.m., CST, weekdays)
FAX : **(317) 895-5298**

CORPORATE ORDERS FOR INTROGRAPHIC BOOKS

Phone: **(800) 469-6616** ext. **206**
(8 a.m.–5 p.m., EST, weekdays)
FAX : **(905) 890-9434**

Qty	ISBN	Title	Price	Total

Shipping & Handling Charges

	Description	First book	Each add'l. book	Total
Domestic	Normal	$4.50	$1.50	$
	Two Day Air	$8.50	$2.50	$
	Overnight	$18.00	$3.00	$
International	Surface	$8.00	$8.00	$
	Airmail	$16.00	$16.00	$
	DHL Air	$17.00	$17.00	$

Subtotal _____

CA residents add
applicable sales tax _____

IN, MA and MD
residents add
5% sales tax _____

IL residents add
6.25% sales tax _____

RI residents add
7% sales tax _____

TX residents add
8.25% sales tax _____

Shipping _____

Total _____

Ship to:

Name _____

Address _____

Company _____

City/State/Zip _____

Daytime Phone _____

Payment: ☐ Check to IDG Books (US Funds Only)
☐ Visa   ☐ Mastercard   ☐ American Express

Card # _____ Exp. _____ Signature _____

IDG Books Education Group
Jim Kelly, Director of Education Sales – 9 Village Circle, Ste. 450, Westlake, TX 76262
800-434-2086 Phone • 817-430-5852 Fax • 8:30-5:00 CST

IDG BOOKS WORLDWIDE REGISTRATION CARD

RETURN THIS REGISTRATION CARD FOR FREE CATALOG

Title of this book: Lotus 1-2-3 R5 Simplified

My overall rating of this book: ❏ Very good [1] ❏ Good [2] ❏ Satisfactory [3] ❏ Fair [4] ❏ Poor [5]

How I first heard about this book:

❏ Found in bookstore; name: [6] _____

❏ Book review: [7] _____

❏ Advertisement: [8] _____

❏ Catalog: [9] _____

❏ Word of mouth; heard about book from friend, co-worker, etc.: [10] _____

❏ Other: [11] _____

What I liked most about this book:

_____

_____

What I would change, add, delete, etc., in future editions of this book:

_____

_____

Other comments:

_____

_____

Number of computer books I purchase in a year: ❏ 1 [12] ❏ 2-5 [13] ❏ 6-10 [14] ❏ More than 10 [15]

I would characterize my computer skills as: ❏ Beginner [16] ❏ Intermediate [17] ❏ Advanced [18] ❏ Professional [19]

I use ❏ DOS [20] ❏ Windows [21] ❏ OS/2 [22] ❏ Unix [23] ❏ Macintosh [24] ❏ Other: [26]_____

(please specify)

I would be interested in new books on the following subjects:

(please check all that apply, and use the spaces provided to identify specific software)

❏ Word processing: [26] _____

❏ Spreadsheets: [27] _____

❏ Data bases: [28] _____

❏ Desktop publishing: [29] _____

❏ File Utilities: [30] _____

❏ Money management: [31] _____

❏ Networking: [32] _____

❏ Programming languages: [33] _____

❏ Other: [34] _____

I use a PC at (please check all that apply): ❏ home [35] ❏ work [36] ❏ school [37] ❏ other: [38] _____

The disks I prefer to use are ❏ 5.25 [39] ❏ 3.5 [40] ❏ other: [41]_____

I have a CD ROM: ❏ yes [42] ❏ no [43]

I plan to buy or upgrade computer hardware this year: ❏ yes [44] ❏ no [45]

I plan to buy or upgrade computer software this year: ❏ yes [46] ❏ no [47]

Name: _____ Business title: [48] _____ Type of Business: [49] _____

Address (❏ home [50] ❏ work [51]/Company name: _____)

Street/Suite# _____

City [52]/State [53]/Zipcode [54]: _____ Country [55] _____

❏ **I liked this book!** You may quote me by name in future IDG Books Worldwide promotional materials.

My daytime phone number is _____

IDG BOOKS

THE WORLD OF COMPUTER KNOWLEDGE

❏ YES!

Please keep me informed about IDG's World of Computer Knowledge.
Send me the latest IDG Books catalog.

BUSINESS REPLY MAIL
FIRST CLASS MAIL   PERMIT NO. 2605   FOSTER CITY, CALIFORNIA

IDG Books Worldwide
919 E Hillsdale Blvd, STE 400
Foster City, CA 94404-9691